# Discovering and Pursuing God's Vision for Your Life

# Discovering and Pursuing God's Vision for Your Life

Designed to Thrive
Book 1

Tyler Drost

**Rise UP**
PUBLICATIONS

ISBN: 978-1-664457-809-4

*Rise UP Publications*
644 Shrewsbury Commons Ave
Ste 249
Shrewsbury PA 17361
United States of America

www.riseUPpublications.com
Phone: 866-846-5123

*For my wife Carolyn, my children Lorelai and Levi, and the people of Thrive Church—thank you for your unwavering support and for walking this journey with me. This work is dedicated to you. May we always run hard after the vision God has given us.*

# Contents

# Introduction

And the Lord answered me:
"Write the vision; make it plain on tablets, so he may
    run who reads it.
For still the vision awaits its appointed time; it
    hastens to the end—it will not lie.
If it seems slow, wait for it; it will surely come; it will
    not delay."

— HABAKKUK 2:2-3 (ESV)

Many people never start running because they lack vision. Consider children—when they are born, they begin by crawling. Then, before you know it, they are stumbling around trying to walk. Somehow, almost overnight, they transition from walking to running.

When people lack vision, they never take that important and vital first step. I often hear people say something like, *I want to get married someday.* But can you truly see yourself being married?

*I want to have a family someday.* Can you envision yourself raising children?

*I want to own a business someday.* Can you see yourself running that business?

*I want to be well in my body.* Can you see yourself well?

Many people never gain momentum because they lack vision. They don't know where they are headed. They have no direction or clear plan for the present, let alone for their future. They have no plans for earthly matters, so how can they have plans for eternity? They go through life hoping things will somehow work out, but without vision, they're stuck. They don't know their destination. Yes, we should pray about our future, but we also need to plan for it. Planning makes vision achievable.

Maybe you feel like life has been moving too slowly, and you've become impatient. Let me encourage you with the Word of God: *"Wait for it."*

*I don't want to hear that, Pastor!*

Well, the Word of God says, *"Wait for it."*

Don't quit. Don't give up. Don't settle. Don't lower your standards.

I've heard a young woman say, *I'm waiting for a godly man who lives in the shadow of the cross.* But after a few months, she settled for a guy with a cross tattoo. Isn't it funny how quickly we compromise when we don't want to wait?

Don't lower your standards. You have come too far to give up now.

Wait for it. Why? Because God says, *"It will surely come. It will not delay."*

## Introduction

Waiting is working. In the church world, we've taught people that it's wrong to wait. I have a six-year-old daughter and a three-year-old son, and their patience is about as long as a hangnail on my pinky. Sometimes I think, 'I wish they'd have some patience.'

Have you ever considered that God in Heaven feels the same way about us? The same things you wish for your children—patience and the ability to wait for a moment—God desires for you and me? Maybe God has perfect timing for everything and a perfect season for each thing, and He says to Himself, *Oh, I wish they would take me at my Word when my Word says, "Wait for it, and it will surely come to pass."*

*I don't want to wait.*

Well, we need to do our part, not just want it to pass.

Waiting is working. But how should we approach waiting? What does waiting involve? That's what this book is about. Let's dig in!

# Chapter One

## Vision Is Seeing into The Invisible

### You Need a Vision for Your Life

Vision is the ability to see beyond what is visible and recognize what has yet to happen. Can you believe God will give you eyes of faith to see things—not as they are, but as they will be in Jesus' name?

Four years ago, when we first moved into our current church building, it looked nothing like it does today. The windows were broken. A hose ran through the building and out the back door, solely to flush the toilet, which connected to plumbing that went nowhere. A tree was literally growing through the roof of the building next door. I'm not exaggerating—there were six separate rooms in the sanctuary space where we now meet.

Believe it or not, there used to be a pink toilet and a green toilet that opened directly into the sanctuary. There was no stage and no lighting. The ceiling was so low that some taller people had to duck to avoid hitting their heads. There were no doors, no ramps, and none of the amenities we have today.

The truth is, four years ago, we didn't have much. We started from humble beginnings.

Do you remember what happened in 2020 during the COVID-19 pandemic? The world shut down. We had nothing—no money, no followers, and no social media presence. And to top it off, a state trooper stopped by and asked, "Would you guys tape up the windows so people stop calling? You're not supposed to be working."

We didn't have much, but we had a vision and had received a Word from God. That's what kept us going. Let's be honest—a Word from God doesn't always come easy or pay the bills right away.

But I stood on that Word. I declared, "God, I believe all things are possible for those who believe. I see this building redeemed. I see doors where there are none, new windows, insulation, and a brand-new HVAC system. I see lights, cameras, chairs, and people. I see action. I see this place renovated and paid for."

And God has done amazing things! We completely renovated the space, restored the old parsonage, and transformed the building next door—one floor at a time.

It's not just about sticks and bricks—it's about the vision. It takes me back to four years ago, when we had nothing but faith, when we saw not what was, but what could be.

## Do You Have a Vision for Your Life?

What does your future look like? What do you envision?

I had lunch with a preacher friend from West Virginia, and I told him, "I believe we're entering a season where God is rebuilding many things in this country. I'm not talking about politics—I'm talking about a great spiritual renewal. I believe we're poised for a time of outpouring. I don't see this as a short-term revival. In my spirit, I feel like we're stepping into a twelve-year season."

He looked straight at me and asked, "So what are you doing about it?"

I told him, "I'm looking ahead. I'm asking myself: What will my family be like in twelve years? What will our ministry look like? What can I do today that will have a big impact on tomorrow?"

That's called having vision.

The truth is, when you have vision, you can turn pain into purpose. You aren't influenced by what people say, how things look, or by your emotions. Instead, you are driven by what you see—what God has revealed to you.

That's why, when God called Abram out of his homeland, He told him, *"Look up. What do you see?"*

Abraham responded, *"I see stars—more than I can count."*

And God said, "So shall your descendants be."

God was showing Abraham a vision of his future. Look up—your redemption draws near.

## Vision Requires Faith

Four years ago, we didn't have much, but we had a vision. I told one of our media team members that our theme song could have been *"High Hopes."* We didn't have a dime, but we always had a vision.

Perhaps you feel like you don't have much. Maybe you feel like you have nothing. But if all you have is a vision, that is enough for God to work through you. God can use you. He can use me. He can use all of us—if we are willing to work together for His kingdom. Vision is about seeing into the invisible because often, you must see it before you can receive it.

Thank God for His grace. God's grace had a vision for you and me when we were messed up. When we were lost in sin, His grace rescued us—not as we were, but as He saw we could be. *"But God shows His love for us in that while we were still sinners, Christ died for us"* (Romans 5:8 ESV). God had a vision for you. He has a vision for this world. He is redeeming all things to Himself.

Nehemiah was an Old Testament figure. He wasn't a pastor, prophet, or miracle worker; he was simply an ordinary guy. Yet, God gave him a vision.

The year was 444 BC. Nehemiah was in exile under the Persian Empire, serving as the king's cupbearer—the lowest position he could hold. His role was simple: taste the king's wine first, and if it were poisoned, he would die. It wasn't exactly a glamorous career with a bright future.

But amid slavery and captivity, he receives a vision from God. Nehemiah refuses to let his circumstances limit what God wants to do through him. He receives his vision from God and carries it out.

> "They said to me, 'Those who survived the exile and are back in the province are in great trouble and disgrace. The wall of Jerusalem is broken down, and its gates have been burned with fire.' When I heard these things, I sat down and wept. For some days, I mourned and fasted and prayed before the God of heaven."
>
> — Nehemiah 1:3-4

When Nehemiah received the news, he wept. But here's what I want to encourage you with: Many times, a vision from God is born out of brokenness. God can take your greatest hurt, your greatest habit, or your greatest hardship—and use it for His glory.

God will redeem you from the very thing that the enemy is using to destroy you. Perhaps you were addicted to drugs—but that's not who you are anymore. Maybe your marriage failed—but now God is using you to help others. Perhaps your business collapsed—but now God is teaching you how to rebuild. God takes our brokenness and turns it into purpose.

What I love about God's children is that they can be knocked down, but they are never knocked out. You can try to defeat them, but they will rise again.

Think about it—throughout the Bible, God's people were enslaved, taken into captivity, and torn from their land. Yet, the incredible thing about God's children is that they don't just survive; they thrive. No matter where they are, even in foreign nations and among unbelievers, they continue to make a significant impact.

Look at Joseph—he was thrown into a pit, sold into slavery, and wrongfully imprisoned; yet, he rose to power as second-in-command over Egypt. Look at Daniel—taken from his homeland as a young man, his enemies repeatedly tried to discredit and destroy him; yet, every time they plotted against him, God elevated him. He went from a captive to a trusted advisor in the kingdom.

Both Joseph and Daniel were enslaved in foreign nations. If God was faithful to them during their captivity, He will surely be faithful to you today.

## What Frustrates You Might Be What You're Called to Fix

Have you ever felt frustrated and complained, *Why doesn't someone do something about this?* Maybe that someone is you.

*Well, how do I know if I'm complaining, Pastor?* It's pretty simple—if all you do is talk about what's wrong without trying to fix it, you're just adding fuel to the fire. Instead of complaining like anyone else could, why not pray, "God, I thank You for giving me a burden for this. Maybe You want to use me to help solve it. Please show me how I can make a difference." Be part of the solution.

God is looking for men and women who will step up and say, "Here I am, Lord. Use me." Is that you?

# Chapter Two

## Frustration Creates Passion

### What Can You Do?

I love that Nehemiah wasn't burdened by what had been. Instead of being stuck in frustration over the past, he turned to God and asked, *"What can I do for the future? I don't want to be like everyone else who just complains. Help me be part of the solution. Help me be the change I want to see. Use me. Give me a vision, a burden, a passion— whatever it takes—to make a kingdom impact, not just blend in with the crowd of complainers."*

What do you do when your expectations are high but your situation seems low, creating a big gap between the two? That gap is where vision plays a role.

You might be looking at something that represents your expectations, but your current reality appears quite different. *How do I get from point A to point B?* you ask. That's where God's vision bridges the gap. His vision anoints you to make a difference and propels you forward.

It wasn't the broken walls that made Nehemiah weep—it was the broken people. Nehemiah's heart wasn't broken over bricks and mortar; it was broken for the people who were now exposed, unprotected, and vulnerable.

## Jesus Is the Only Hope for the World

When people give their time or treasure at Thrive Church, Honesdale, it's not about sticks and bricks. It's about the mission—to bring hope to the broken people by telling them that Jesus is the hope of the world.

We believe that Jesus is the only hope for the world. We know whom we have believed in. We have a vision to see people reconciled to God. We envision lives being transformed. We believe God can do anything, at any time, in any place.

We aspire to be His hands and feet, reaching out to those far from God. Our vision is to make a difference in our region—and far beyond.

## Are You Burdened by What Burdens God?

Ask yourself this: Am I burdened by the same things that burden God? Or have I become so spiritually desensitized that all I care about is myself? My money. My family. My job. My comfort. Have I become a "me monster"—when the gospel is quite the opposite?

What burdens God? People far from Him who are dying and going to Hell. How do I know this? *"The Lord is not willing that any should perish but that all should come to repentance"* (2 Peter 3:9 NKJV). It is God's will for everyone to be saved. But not everyone receives salvation.

Why?

Because of the gap—the space where people make their own choices. I wish everyone would go to Heaven, don't you? It would be much easier. But the truth is, not everyone chooses Him. And that breaks God's heart.

We should be the ones burdened by what burdens God, individuals who say, "I want to go beyond with my giving, my living, and every area of my life."

We should be the people who realize this isn't about me; it's about God's vision—about advancing His kingdom. And if you want to be part of God's blessing, you must also be part of His burden.

## Waiting on God's Timing

Nehemiah foreshadows Jesus. In the New Testament, we see Jesus weeping over Jerusalem because the people are broken and lost. Nehemiah receives a vision, but what does he do next? He waits.

Maybe you're thinking, *I don't want to wait! This is America! I want it my way, and I want it yesterday. I want Burger King Christianity—my way, right away!*

We often receive a vision from God and mistakenly assume it requires immediate action. *Aren't you going to do something now?* However, Scripture says, *"Wait on the Lord."* Why? Because waiting teaches us to trust God's timing.

*But I don't like the process! I want things instantly—microwaved, not slow-cooked!* you say.

The truth is, there's nothing worse than receiving the right thing at the wrong time. Many people step into a God-given vision too soon. And what happens? It's like giving birth prematurely—it's weak, malnourished, and not fully developed. Why? Because you rushed ahead of God instead of trusting His timing.

*I just want to get it done!* you exclaim.

I'm not saying you shouldn't move when God calls you to move, but you need to understand timing and seasons. You can't be all gas and no brakes—otherwise, you'll drive yourself right off a cliff.

Nehemiah waited four months. Thank God he wasn't like Moses—Moses waited 40 years!

Joseph had a dream at seventeen, and he had to wait twenty years for it to come true.

David was anointed king, yet had to spend years as a shepherd, waiting for his time.

But I find reassurance in what Isaiah 40 says:

> But those who wait on the Lord
> Shall renew their strength;
> They shall mount up with wings like eagles,
> They shall run and not be weary,
> They shall walk and not faint.
>
> — Isaiah 40:31 (NKJV)

Nehemiah's story shows that God can give purpose to any season. Even during your time as a cupbearer—especially when you feel stuck—God has a purpose for you right where you are.

You don't need to be a pastor, a shouter, or a dancer. You just need to be a child of God.

## God Has a Vision for Every Season of Your Life

You might feel like an ordinary person working a regular job, but God can use you. He can take any season and turn it into something for His glory because God has a vision for every season of your life.

Be faithful today—not *"someday."* A vision rarely requires immediate action; it mostly requires patience.

Some people say, *Rome wasn't built in a day.* Someone else says, *Well, if I were the foreman, it would have been!*

Learn to wait on the Lord. Don't race ahead of God. However, you also don't want to fall behind. You need to stay in step with His voice and the leading of the Holy Spirit.

Our goal as a church has never been to become a large congregation. The aim is to reach those far from God. Has the church grown? Yes. God is moving by His Spirit, and He alone deserves the glory. However, growth is simply a byproduct of health. It's not about becoming a megachurch—it's about being a soul-winning church. It's about people finding forgiveness, hope, mercy, purpose, and true life in Christ Jesus.

Most people dislike waiting because they are eager to start working. But God says: Waiting is working. If God has promised something and I wait on Him, He will always deliver. That's who our God is.

## Be Faithful Where You Are

I meet young people who say, *When I get to preach, then things are going to be good.* They've missed the whole point. It's not about who's holding the microphone—it's about who's holding the ladder.

Youthful ambition sometimes says, *I'm going to be a great evangelist.* Really? What are you doing now?

I hear it all the time—people telling me what they will be someday when they get their chance. But what are you doing where you're at now? Jesus said, *"When you've been faithful with little, then I will entrust you with much"* (Matthew 25:23 ESV).

How about being faithful where you are? Be faithful in your school, in your workplace, and in the influence and favor God has given you. Don't just dream about what you'll do someday; start sowing the seeds now. Someday never comes unless you start today. Waiting is working.

If God has made a promise, I've learned that when I wait on Him, He always delivers. The greater the responsibility, the more preparation is required. Yet, many people fail to prepare. They don't plan. *I'm just going to do this,* they say. No, you're preparing to fail.

Proper planning prevents poor performance. People tell me *I'm twenty-five years old. Why do I need to start saving for retirement? Why do I need to start investing?* Oh, Dave Ramsey would have a heart attack right now. *I'm just going to live my life.* Sure—but then you'll be broke at twenty-five, broke at thirty-five, and broke at forty-five. And you'll blame God for it.

What are you doing about it today?

*Well, God's going to…* Stop blaming God—what are you doing? Are you praying as if everything depends on Him while working as if everything depends on you? Or are you just pipe-dreaming? Because a vision without a plan is nothing but a dream. I don't want to hear about someday. What are you doing today to make tomorrow different?

Make a plan. If you're going to do something, plan for it and follow through. Pray about it—but also plan for it.

## Stop Using "Led by the Spirit" as an Excuse for Laziness

Some people don't plan at all. Instead, they say, *Oh, I'm just led by the Spirit.* No, you're not. You're lazy. Don't blame God for your lack of planning and disorganization. Do you really think the Holy Spirit, the all-knowing, all-powerful God, can't plan? He is the Alpha and the Omega—the beginning and the end. He wrote this entire Bible—completely inspired and without error. Do you think He can't plan for Tuesday?

What does your vision look like for next year? What about for next month? I'm not saying everything always follows the plan. I wish it would. It doesn't.

Are you just as broke this year as you were last year, blaming the economy and everyone else for your poor decisions? *Well, the cost of everything has gone up!* I agree. But have you made any changes? Or are you still stuck in the same hole as last year?

I met with a friend and told him, "Here's what I'm believing for. Here's how I'm going to make my kids' future better than mine. Here's how I'm going to improve the ministry. Here's how we're going to grow."

He was stunned. Why? Because we have a history of accepting things as they are while simultaneously believing, "God, I believe this is what it could be. God, I believe this is where You're calling us to go. God, I believe You are going to build this thing, grow this thing, and move this thing forward. I believe You're going to do the impossible."

And when the vision is fulfilled, people will look at it and only be able to say, "It had to be the hand of God." There's no other way it could have happened.

## If Life Gets Too Hard to Stand, Kneel

While we wait, what should we do? If life becomes too hard to stand, kneel. Avoid gossiping. Stop posting on Facebook. Before you start talking about it—I hope you've prayed about it.

My wife, Carolyn, is originally from Montreal, Quebec. Over ten years ago, we started the immigration process in this country, which, anyone who has gone through knows, is a nightmare.

We got married a little over ten years ago. Everything was great. We started the process for her permanent residency, following the steps and doing everything by the book.

About a month into our marriage, we received our first letter in the mail from our beloved government. By that time, we had already filed for her permanent residency. It had cost us a lot of money, along with countless hours of paperwork and stress.

That letter stated, "You have to pay X amount of dollars and refile, or she has 30 days to leave the country."

It happened again.

And again.

And again.

I'll never forget being in our small farmhouse kitchen. I was working four jobs just to keep us afloat. We did everything we could—signed away benefits, sacrificed every penny, filled out forms, and followed every rule. And still, the government kept blocking us. Sitting there in that kitchen, exhausted and burned out, I said, "God, we're trying to do things the right way. Lord, you've used me greatly at a young age. I've preached this message. Signs, wonders, and miracles have taken place. I've seen Your hand at work in my life. But God, I don't know what else to say. I've had enough."

Have you ever been there before? *God, this thing is killing us. I'm exhausted—financially, emotionally, mentally.*

Think about it—this was our first year of marriage.

*God, I don't know what else to do. I'm literally working four jobs. We're serving in the church. We're doing everything we can to be a blessing to Your kingdom. But God, what else do I do?*

I sat at the kitchen table, cracked open my Bible, and read:

> So Jesus answered and said to them, "Have faith in
> God. For assuredly, I say to you, whoever says to
> this mountain, 'Be removed and be cast into the
> sea,' and does not doubt in his heart, but believes
> that those things he says will be done, he will
> have whatever he says. Therefore I say to
> you, whatever things you ask when you pray,
> believe that you receive them, and you will
> have them.
>
> — Mark 11:22-24 (NKJV)

I said, "Either this works, or it doesn't. Either God is who He says He is—or He's not."

*But you're a preacher!* you say.

Yeah, I am. But I'm also honest. At that moment, I confessed it. I believed God. I prayed. And when I couldn't stand anymore, I got on my knees. I didn't know what else to do. "God, I've had enough. We've been waiting long enough, and I don't know what else to do."

For three days—what felt like the longest three days of my life—we had no idea what was coming next. Would it be another letter stating we owed an additional $10,000? Would it be another denial? Would she receive another thirty-day warning to leave the country?

Then, on the third day, Carolyn got a call from our immigration lawyer asking, "What are you guys into?"

Carolyn was confused by the question. "What do you mean? What are we *into*?"

The lawyer replied, "For the last three nights, every time I've gone to sleep, I keep having the same dream over and over again. But this dream is crazy."

Carolyn asked, "What is it?"

The lawyer explained, "In the dream, I called a state senator's office, and they patched me through to him. The senator then called immigration in Philadelphia and demanded that your case be overturned. I keep waking up with this dream, and I have no idea why."

Carolyn calmly responded, "Well, we believe God speaks through dreams and visions."

At that point, I was desperate. I hoped it was God—because I had nothing else. I had burned through all my savings. We had nothing left.

Then the lawyer asked, "How are you going to get a state senator on the phone? Have you ever tried to reach a politician?"

She called the senator's office, expecting nothing. But he answered the phone and recognized my name. "Is that the young preacher I've seen on television? Because for the last two weeks, at 5:00 AM, I've been watching that young man, and I really like what he has to say."

This state senator—whom I had never met—called immigration and demanded that Carolyn's case be overturned. Within seven days, we received a letter in the mail: Her permanent residency had been approved.

Fast forward—Carolyn applied for naturalization to become a U.S. citizen. She studied 200 questions for her test. We went to Philadelphia. She aced it—because God was with her. Then they told us it would take 90 to 120 days before we received an answer.

It was a Wednesday night, and Carolyn had taken the kids to church. I did what I usually do—I went out back, sat by the fire, looked at the stars, and just said, "God, You've been so good to us."

At 8:30 PM, my security camera sent me an alert. It was the mail lady, which was unusual because she usually came at 5:30 PM. I opened the door.

"Sorry, this letter—it seemed important. I just felt like I needed to bring it back to you tonight."

I thanked her, took it, walked inside, looked down, and saw the U.S. Immigration seal. Carolyn's approval had arrived. We were heading to Philadelphia for her swearing-in ceremony. After ten years, the wait was finally over.

What have I learned about waiting? If I wait, He's working. If I just believe, He's working. When He said, "Wait for it," it will surely come. How's it going to happen? I don't know. It's not my job to figure it out. I don't want to mess it up. I don't want to rush ahead of it. I don't want to interfere. I want to wait in faith and believe He's going to do it. I want to do what He told me to do.

If life becomes too hard to stand, it's time to kneel. Before you start posting on Facebook—before you discuss it, pray about it.

# Chapter Three

## Prayer Keeps a Vision Alive

### Prayer Connects Our Heart to God's

Prayer keeps a vision alive by connecting our hearts to God's heart. Your vision develops through prayer, which is why staying connected to Him is essential.

Many people believe they have the full vision when they only have a part of it. Then, they jump into action while God is saying, "I just showed you a scene. Let me show you the whole movie." You're operating based on the trailer, and God wants to reveal the entire film—but the only way to see it is to keep digging the well.

Keep returning to the well through prayer. Continue to align your heart with His and say, "God, I thank You for what You did, but now I want more. God, I thank You that the vision is going to keep expanding because I'm going to keep seeing it through prayer."

I firmly believe this: A pastor sees and establishes the vision, but the body of Christ—the church—determines the speed at which the vision is accomplished.

As a pastor, I need to keep returning to the well in prayer, and you must do the same. We all need to keep digging this well. We should say, "God, I thank You for showing me the trailer, but I want the whole three-hour movie. I want the beginning, the middle, and the end. I don't want just one scene. God, I don't want to run ahead of You."

Do you realize how difficult it is for a man of faith—a pastor, a visionary leader—to say, "I'm willing to wait"? That is one of the most challenging things you could tell someone like me. It demands great obedience and perseverance.

Anyone can run recklessly off a cliff—dragging others along with them. But it takes a true man or woman of God to humble themselves and say, "You know what, Lord? I have faith to run, but I also have enough faith to wait. I have enough faith to trust You. I have enough faith to trust Your process and Your timing. I don't understand it, but I know Your ways are higher than my ways. I know Your thoughts are not my thoughts."

## Prayer Helps You See What You Would Otherwise Miss

If you want to get married, I recommend spending some time in prayer about it. Some people rush into it, saying, "Yeah, she's the one." Then, after four relationships, they're still saying the same thing. You're getting ahead of God, and you're missing it.

*Yes, but I'm in a hurry.*

Why? Slow down. Take a deep breath. It's okay. It's not a sprint; it's a marathon. We have an entire race set before us.

Now, there are situations where it's good to move quickly. For example, our church has a Vision Sunday once a year. It's a time when we go above and beyond in generosity to move the church's vision forward. In these cases, I know there are things God wants us to accomplish quickly. But I also know there are times when God says, "Slow down on that." And that's when I step back and say, "Yes, Sir. I'm Yours to command."

Everything we've done as a church has aimed to stay in step with God. Are we perfect? No. But we strive to follow what the Lord is saying and doing.

I don't want to run ahead of Him. Too many people want to run without purpose. I don't want to be like that. Am I hustling? Yes. Waiting isn't an excuse to be lazy—I want to stay in step with Him and fulfill what He has called us to do.

Why? Is it for our church to experience explosive growth overnight? No. It is so we can stay healthy, grow steadily, and keep advancing in what God has called us to do.

## Vision Starts with a Burden

Nehemiah feels a heavy burden for what has happened, and from this burden comes a strong passion for what could be. The first thing he does is drop to his knees and pray.

May we be people who wait on the Lord and learn to trust Him and His timing.

*But, I don't like His timing.*

Well, God is always on time. He's never early—that's for sure—and He's never late. He's always on time.

If we say we have great faith, then we need to prove ourselves by humbling ourselves and saying, "Lord, I'm going to trust You and wait on Your timing. You showed me where we're headed in the future, what we're going to do, but I'm going to be faithful where I am. I'm going to be faithful where You've called me. I'll be fruitful where You've placed me. You'll take me where You want me to go—that's up to You. I trust You and Your timing."

That's why I don't go around constantly announcing what I'm going to do next. I don't need to because those things are between me and God. My job is to be faithful where I am. My job is to prosper where I'm planted.

Someone once asked me why I was in Honesdale when I could be anywhere else. They thought I was crazy. I told them I was exactly where God wanted me to be, but they didn't understand.

They don't need to understand because I'm waiting on Him. I'm trusting His process and timing, believing that He who began a good work in us is faithful to complete it in Christ Jesus.

> "Lord, let your ear be attentive to the prayer of this
> your servant and to the prayer of your servants
> who delight in revering your name. Give your
> servant success today by granting him favor in the
> presence of this man."
> I was cupbearer to the king.
>
> — Nehemiah 1:11

## Pray for an Opportunity

I told you before, the cupbearer's job was to taste the king's wine before he drank it. I'm sure the wine was exceptionally good. However, the problem with that job is that many people want to poison the king. If the wine is poisoned, the cupbearer dies, and the king moves on—"Get us a new cupbearer!" That's why it was one of the lowest jobs in the kingdom.

But here's the thing about God's kingdom—He's always turning things upside down. What seems like it should work one way, God flips over.

Consider this: "Give, and it will be given to you." That's not how things work here in the visible realm. However, in the kingdom of God, everything is counterintuitive.

So what does Nehemiah do? The first thing he does is pray for an opportunity. He says, "Lord, let your ear be attentive."

When was the last time you asked God for an opportunity? I'm not talking about, "Oh, God, give me an opportunity to be a millionaire. God, give me an opportunity to win the lottery."

I'm talking about:

*God, give me an opportunity to be a blessing.*

*God, give me an opportunity to witness to someone.*

*God, give me an opportunity to have grace today—so I don't lose my temper with them.*

*God, give me an opportunity to exemplify You today.*

*God, give me an opportunity to be a positive influence in a negative world.*

Many people make excuses, claiming they're waiting for the supernatural instead of asking God for an opportunity to act.

I serve the God of miracles. We've seen Him work, and we know He is a God of the supernatural. But don't use waiting on the supernatural as an excuse for laziness. Don't let it be an excuse to do nothing.

## God Gives Us Opportunities Daily

God gives us opportunities every single day.

How about this—an opportunity to be faithful. Jesus said, *"When you're faithful with little, I'll make you ruler over much"* (Matthew 25:23 ESV).

How about the opportunity to be obedient, like when we return God's tithe to Him? Here's the truth about the tithe—either you return it or you steal it. Either way, it's a choice. It's a choice to be obedient.

Each time we obey, God gives us another opportunity to be faithful. But you and I must walk through the door. If you walk through the door, God will open a whole new world to you. If you're faithful... if you're obedient... And while you're at it, you might as well add patience—because we all dislike waiting. However, God provides us with opportunities every day, often without us realizing it. God offers us chances to be faithful, obedient, and patient.

*Yes, but I don't like patience.*

I told you before—if you're willing to wait, waiting is working.

Scripture says, *"Wait for it; it will surely come"* (Habakkuk 2:3 ESV). We must trust that while we're waiting, He's working.

God grants opportunities every day, but it's up to you and me to step through the door. And when you do, He'll reveal a whole new world to you.

May God grant you an opportunity to be a blessing today.

# Chapter Four

## Vision from God Produces Supernatural Favor

W e were at a friend's place one night—a beautiful farm. I felt so happy for them. You could sense God's presence there. I'm from the countryside, so you must understand—I hate living in a town. I tried city life for a little while when we were in college. But out there in the country, on that farm, my kids wanted to move there. They were running around, playing with the goats, climbing on the John Deere tractor, and messing with the pool table—just being kids. And honestly—I'm a big kid too, and I never want to stop being a kid.

The men sat at a high-top table, talking as men usually do, while the women gathered in another room. We discussed how good God has been—how we saw His favor in our families, businesses, and marriages. "Every good and perfect gift comes down from the Father of lights" (James 1:17).

I looked around at those guys and said, "Look at us. Our wives and kids are here. We're all enjoying each other's company. If it weren't for this house, we wouldn't even know each other." I continued,

"This property is incredible. Look at what God did for you guys. I'm your biggest cheerleader."

We were excited and having a great time that night discussing God's favor because I love witnessing His blessings in people's lives.

Can you see it in every part of your life? Maybe God's favor stepped in when cancer threatened to take your life. Or perhaps God's favor intervened when your marriage seemed headed for divorce. Maybe God's favor arrived when your business was on the brink of bankruptcy and losing everything, but His favor lifted you up and restored you.

## The Favor of God Will Put You in Places You Never Expected

I am amazed at the many ways God has given me favor. Some of the businesspeople I work with aren't Christians. Not yet, anyway. But I believe God put me in their path because I'm going to lead them to Christ. I venture where others aren't willing to go. I don't dismiss people the way others do.

*God, I know You gave me favor with that man for a reason. I know You gave me favor with that family for a reason. I know You placed me here, giving me favor because I will be Jesus' hands and feet.*

I'm not afraid to go where God has called me or to do what He has tasked me with. I'm not backing down.

"Fear tolerated is faith contaminated."

I believe the favor of God makes a way where there is no way.

It's not just about connections with people; it's about gaining favor with God and man. When you adopt God's vision for your life, His favor will bless you in every area—spiritually, physically, financially, relationally, and emotionally.

## Favor Doesn't Force—Favor Flows

Nehemiah prayed for favor, and God added the resources. You don't really need more money—you need more favor. Favor doesn't force things; favor flows.

> And Jesus grew in wisdom and stature, and in favor
> with God and man.
>
> — LUKE 2:52

If Jesus needed favor with God and favor with man, then surely you and I need it even more.

Waiting is working, but while I wait, I'm going to get on my knees in prayer. How about you? I'm not just praying, "Oh, God, I need, I need, I need." I'm praying, "God, give me an opportunity. God, let Your favor increase in my life. God, open doors that no man can shut. God, give me favor to walk through the doors You place in front of me—with ease."

I believe God's favor will open not only what I need but also what I want because favor doesn't force; it flows. I don't want people to see me; I want them to see a child of God, favored by the Lord.

When you have favor, you don't need to promote yourself. When you have favor, you don't have to pursue ambition. When you have favor, there's no need to reveal everything you're doing.

## When You've Been Marked by God, You Don't Have to Market Yourself

One of the worst mistakes you can make is exposing your personal business to everyone—because not everyone is in your corner.

A while ago, someone sent me a rude message at 3:45 AM—hiding behind a blocked number. "Who's this?" I asked. I never heard from them again. Why? Because not everyone appreciates the blessings of God in your life.

But if God has marked you, there isn't a demon in Hell that can stop what God has begun in you.

> He who began a good work in you will be faithful to complete it.
>
> — Philippians 1:6

And once God has marked you, nothing can prevent His favor from flowing into your life.

# Chapter Five

## A Vision Without a Plan Is a Fantasy

### Stop Using Prayer as an Excuse for Laziness

Nehemiah didn't just receive a vision from God—he also received a plan. He not only prayed in faith, trusting that God would act, but he also planned with expectation, believing God would make it happen. Nehemiah loved prayer, but he knew prayer alone wasn't enough. It was now time to develop a plan to achieve the vision.

Some Christians can be strange. Not all of them, but let's be honest—some are. I've met people over the years who say something like, *You know, brother, I'm just called to pray all day.*

"No, you're not," I tell them.

*"What?"* they ask in surprise.

Yes, you should pray every day. But you're not called to sit around and pray *all* day. God called you to work—God is not a socialist.

The Bible says, *"The one who is unwilling to work shall not eat"* (2 Thessalonians 3:10). So get a job. Stop being lazy and blaming God for why you're not working. *God has* called you to pray—but He also called you to be productive.

Let me remind you of the very first command He ever gave: *"Be fruitful and multiply; fill the earth and subdue it"* (Genesis 1:28 NKJV). And guess what? You can't do those things while lounging around on the couch in your stretchy pants, praying all day. Get a job and become a productive citizen; contribute to society.

## Pray, Then Plan

If you genuinely engage in prayer, you should come away with a plan. Don't enter the prayer closet and come out empty-handed. When I pray, I believe God hears me and that He answers me. I also believe that faith without works is dead (James 2:26). You can't have faith without corresponding action.

I don't preach just to have something to do. I preach so people will give their hearts to God. I know faith comes by hearing, and hearing by the Word of God. I believe that, and I'm not ashamed of the gospel, for it is the power of God for salvation. *But how can they hear unless someone preaches?* (Romans 10). Somebody has to get out there and take action.

*Well, I just serve at church.*

You're meant for more than this because you're part of something bigger. That's why I care so much about servant leadership. It helps us reach more people for Jesus together. We're not supposed to be a one-person show. It's about all of us coming together as a unified church to do something great because we have the answer, and His name is Jesus Christ.

After you pray, you should have something to show for it. Many people say they're waiting on God when they're really just wasting the season. Don't waste the waiting season.

Nehemiah prayed and planned. He received a vision from God and started making a plan.

> In the month of Nisan in the twentieth year of King
> Artaxerxes, when wine was brought for him, I
> took the wine and gave it to the king. I had not
> been sad in his presence before, so the king asked
> me, "Why does your face look so sad when you
> are not ill? This can be nothing but sadness of
> heart."
> I was very much afraid, but I said to the king, "May
> the king live forever! Why should my face not
> look sad when the city where my ancestors are
> buried lies in ruins, and its gates have been
> destroyed by fire?"
> The king said to me, "What is it you want?"
>
> — Nehemiah 2:1-4

What if God stepped in front of you and asked, *"What do you want?"* Do you have an answer? Do you have a plan? Vision without a plan is just a fantasy. Nehemiah had both.

What do *you* have?

# Chapter Six

## Is Your Vision Prepared?

### Are You Prepared to Answer?

If God asked you what you want, would you be prepared to answer Him? Or does your vision lack preparation? Are you disorganized and lazy, telling yourself, *"Oh, I'm just led by the Spirit"*?

God is the Master Planner. Don't blame God for being disorganized. Don't blame Him for avoiding what He has called you to do. What do you want?—Are you ready to answer?

### The Night God Challenged My Faith

A few years ago, I experienced a serious problem with my eyesight. I went from 20/20 vision to near blindness.

I saw several doctors. They told me, "There's nothing you can do. You're going blind." As the days went on, my eyes swelled so much that I could barely see. I'd go out and preach, and miracles would happen. But after the service, Carolyn had to drive me home— because I could barely see my hand in front of my face.

Nobody else knew. During this time, I was laying hands on people, and miracles were taking place—yet I could barely see.

One night, Carolyn was driving us home while I sat in the passenger seat, believing for a miracle and trusting in my healing—but in the natural, nothing was changing. Then, as clear as day, I heard God speak: "What do you want?"

I said, "I'm glad You asked. I have a list right here on my phone." And I did. I said, "Here's what I'm believing for." Now, God already knew my list, but I believe He was testing my faith. I mentioned the biggest item on the list—something that would have turned the church world upside down. Then God said to me, "Is that all I can do? Take the limits off Me."

## Taking the Limits Off God

I am a blessed man. But in that moment in the car, I felt convicted. I said, "Okay, God—you want me to believe You for more? I'll believe You for it. I believe You can do it. I don't know how it will happen. It would have to be You. And I know it's going to make people gnash their teeth at me. But I'll tell You right now—if You do it, I've got no problem receiving it. And You know I'll give You the glory for it—every bit of it. Okay, limits are off."

I deleted what I had previously written on my phone and wrote something much larger.

The next day, I was at a service, playing the piano while Ted Shuttlesworth Sr[1] preached. He turned to me and said, "Sing."

---

1. Ted Shuttlesworth Sr. is a Pentecostal evangelist and founder of Faith Alive Ministries. He is widely known for his healing ministry, tent revivals, and emphasis on miracles, faith, and the power of the Holy Spirit in evangelism. His ministry has reached people across the U.S. and internationally.

I tried to pass it off with a joke.

"I'm serious," he persisted. "Sing."

I'll never forget the song he told me to sing—an old Andraé Crouch song, "Let the Church Say Amen." I sang it and led the church in that song, even though it sounded terrible. But I did it anyway; I was obedient.

Now, Brother Ted didn't understand what I was going through. He said to me, "You were just given an opportunity to be obedient, and you took it. But what I was really doing was building your faith for something. You haven't told anybody—but you've been going blind in your eyes. Tonight, the Lord heals your eyes."

That night, the Lord healed my eyes. I went back to my eye doctor, and he confirmed that my vision was 20/20. That was over four years ago.

## Ask for What You Want, Not Just What You Need

Why would God do something like that? I believe it was because when God asked me—*"What do you want?"*—I was ready to answer Him. I had not been praying for the things I need because I don't need to. That might sound like arrogance, but it's actually confidence. It's confidence in what God has already said: "My God shall supply all my needs according to His riches in glory by Christ Jesus" (Philippians 4:19 NKJV). So why would I ask God for something He already promised to provide?

Instead of praying about my *needs*, I pray about my *wants*. I pray, *"God, here's what I want..."* That idea might rub people the wrong way.

But the truth is, God said, *"Delight yourself in the Lord, and He will give you the desires of your heart"* (Psalm 37:4 ESV). Therefore, I don't pray about what I need; I pray about what I want.

God, I want to be used greater in the anointing.

God, I want to be used greater in the gifts of the Spirit.

God, I want to advance Your kingdom.

Why? Because I already know He will take care of my needs. He has given me the principles of seedtime and harvest. I sow, and He takes care of it. We've never lacked a day in our lives.

Simply put, if you follow what He has told you to do, you could delete most of your prayer lists. You wouldn't need to be a lifelong prayer project.

*I just need money.*

No, you don't. What you need is more of God's favor in your life. He's already given you money. The Scripture says in 2 Corinthians 9:10, "He has given seed to the sower." But you haven't sown your seed; you've been eating your seed, and now you're wondering why you don't have enough money.

Most people are their own problem. You need to mature, stop being lazy, and become a productive citizen. Don't ask God about your needs; tell Him what you want.

The list I had that night in the car didn't include any needs; they were all wants. A church isn't a need. It's something God desires. I said, *"God, we want to do this because it's Your vision. We don't need to do this. We want to because we want to advance Your kingdom beyond where we are now."*

## Vision Requires Preparation

Nehemiah was ready when the king asked him what he wanted.

> And I answered the king, "If it pleases the king and if
> your servant has found favor in his sight, let him
> send me to the city in Judah where my ancestors
> are buried so that I can rebuild it."

> — Nehemiah 2:5

Nehemiah didn't have just a one-step plan. He came out of the prayer closet with a detailed plan from God—one that unfolded over the next seven chapters. Nehemiah prepared himself in faith for the day when the king would ask him, "What do you want?" With your prayer, faith, and preparation, start getting ready for the day when God asks you: "Hey, son, what do you want?"

## Nehemiah's 7-Step Plan That Came from His Time in Prayer

Step One: Hey King, can I go back to Jerusalem?

Imagine this—a slave standing before the king and making this request. And not just any slave—a cupbearer. In those days, the king could have executed him on the spot just for asking.

Step Two: I don't have any money. Can you fund this expedition?

Nehemiah lacked resources and needed the king's financial support to accomplish this.

Step Three: A lot of people hate my race, King. Can you give me letters of authority?

He knew opposition was approaching. He needed official letters from the king to prove his right to be there.

Step Four: Hey King, can I talk to Asaph—the guy who runs your forest?

Nehemiah knew exactly who to turn to for his particular needs.

Now, let's connect the dots: Nehemiah has no money. He needs a letter of authority to request supplies. The king must permit him to return to the land they overthrew. And now, he's going to ask the person who manages the king's forest—who likely despises him and his people—to provide all the lumber he needs.

But Nehemiah believed that God was at work. He knew that God would grant him favor with the king, favor with the lumberyard, and favor every step of the journey. Because if God wasn't working, he would be dead.

Step Five: Hey, King, can you make me governor of Jerusalem?

He needed the remnant to recognize his authority so they would listen to him.

Step Six: Hey, King, can I gather all the Hebrew people?

He needed to cast the vision, explaining what breaks God's heart, and delegate authority so they could accomplish the mission.

Step Seven: Now, let's build something.

Many of us get a vision and immediately say, "Let's build!" but we often skip the previous steps.

## Come Out of the Prayer Closet with a Plan

*God, I need a job.*

No—God, grant me an opportunity for a job. Grant me favor. So when they ask, *Why should I hire you?* you'll be ready with, *I'm glad you finally asked.*

*Why should I give you money?* I'm glad you asked—I currently have 100 reasons with me. If you need 150, I'll return to my prayer closet to gather some more.

*Why should I let you marry my daughter?* Because I have a vision and a plan.

Are you prepared if God were to ask you: *What do you want?* Or is your vision lacking preparation?

# Chapter Seven

## A Vision Without a Plan Is Useless

### What's Your Plan?

E ven with vision, great ideas often fail each day because of poor planning.

My brother and I run a sanitation company together. We regularly set a vision: "Here's where we want to be by January 1, the number of customers we're believing for, the trucks we want on the road, the support equipment we'll need, and a plan to make it happen."

*It's just a sanitation company,* some might say. *How hard could it be?*

Although it might appear simple, we don't take the business lightly. We have a vision from God for our business, not just a dream—we have a plan to bring it to fruition.

Often, people say, *I have a vision to be in ministry.* Are you sure? What's your plan? Who are you serving? Where are you serving? Or are you just waiting for an evangelist to show up, call you out, and hand you a microphone? How about creating a plan and beginning to work toward something?

My church has a plan to "accelerate the vision" by uniting people, praying, and seeking God's guidance. We're not concerned about paying for buildings—that's already handled. We're moving forward with the vision God has given us.

I've been praying, "God, what do You want me to do personally to lead the way in accelerating the vision?" I don't mention this to boast—I say it humbly; I take the initiative here. I am seeking a personal plan for my role in this vision because leaders lead the way. Don't call yourself a leader if you're not leading anyone. If you're a leader, turn around and look behind you—who's following you? What impact are you making? Are you leading in key areas? Or do you simply enjoy the title without embracing the responsibilities?

## A Vision Without a Plan Is Just a Dream

Vision without a plan is useless. I strongly believe this: The pastor envisions and establishes the vision, but the church determines the pace at which the vision is achieved.

In December 2022, we moved into our current building; however, just two years earlier, it was a disaster. It probably should have been demolished with a bulldozer; the building next door was even worse. But I had a vision for what it could become—I could see it. As I mentioned before, our theme song should have been *High Hopes* because we didn't have a dime, but we had a vision.

The first thing we did was transform the interior space into a single open area because I knew we would grow and quickly need more room. Many people didn't understand my vision for having more space with so few people initially. Yet, I envisioned the place filled. Others were quick to point out that we didn't have enough money. But when you tell me what I lack, I'll share what I have. I know in Whom I have believed. I have a vision, and I can turn it into a plan and write it down.

## From a Wreck to a House of Worship

The windows were broken, the plumbing was a garden hose, the furnace was a relic from the 1960s, the roof leaked everywhere, and there was no insulation. I consulted a builder and planner who has worked on projects all over for assistance. He listened intently as I explained my vision and agreed to help.

We outlined the pricing for everything. I clearly presented the vision. Then, we started trusting God to supply all we needed.

There were times when we had no money and times when we had no people. I didn't even have a place to preach. But I stood firm and prayed, "God, this is Your vision. I've done my homework. I've made the plan. I don't know how it's going to happen, but I trust that while I'm waiting, You're working."

## Faith Requires Action

At the end of 2020, we started the church in a rented building while we worked on our own facility. That brought its own set of challenges.

Renting a facility like that was incredibly expensive. The utilities? You wouldn't believe how much they added up to. There were months when Carolyn and I handled everything ourselves because we had to. We'd receive an offering—maybe $700 for the night— and we'd give $500 of it to the building owner, week after week. But I knew God had called us. I knew God had given us a vision.

One night, I stood in the place where I now preach and said, "God, if I have to sell my house, it's Yours. If I have to move into a one-bedroom apartment, I will. This is Your vision. I have a plan. I don't know how it's going to work, but I'm all in." I'm not sharing this to brag. I'm sharing it because I've witnessed the faithfulness of God.

## God Expanded His Church

God saved and healed people, filling them with the Holy Spirit. People were obedient in giving their tithes and offerings. This ministry has touched people all over the world, leading them to join us as partners online, saying, *"Pastor, I don't just want to be a spectator—I want to be a participant."*

The pastor sees and sets the vision, but the church determines the speed at which it's accomplished. This is what I felt God gave us:

- Jesus is our message.
- People are our heart.
- Excellence is our spirit.
- Generosity is our privilege.
- Honor is our calling.
- Servant leadership is our identity.
- Passion is our pursuit.
- God is making a way. And we're walking in it.

## Three Things That Make a Good Plan

1. Make it simple and clear for people.
2. Guide people through the process.
3. Give people confidence that they're making the right decision.

When reading the Old Testament and studying God's Word, we're not just searching for principles; we're discovering a person—Jesus Christ, our Savior and Lord. The truth is, there has never been a better planner than our Father in Heaven.

## Surround Yourself with Wise Counsel

Someone once told me, *All the guys on your board are older. You need younger people.* I'm less concerned with age than I am with productivity, experience, and commitment.

Every man on my board is a person of integrity, still married, financially stable, spiritually mature, and able to make wise decisions. They also serve as mentors, guiding me because they've traveled the same road I'm on now.

The late Jerry Sevell[1] preached at our dedication service. We had coffee the next morning. Sitting across from me, he looked at me and said, "I can't figure you out."

I laughed.

Brother Jerry continued, "With the connections you have, you could invite anyone to preach at your church. So why do you only bring in guys like me and Ted Shuttlesworth?"

I told him, "Brother Jerry, I don't know how much longer you'll be on this Earth. I want to learn everything I can from you and from these men of God who have paved the way."

---

1. Jerry Savelle (1946–2024) was a respected author, teacher, and founder of Jerry Savelle Ministries International. A protégé of Kenneth Copeland, he was known for preaching faith, favor, and financial prosperity in the life of the believer. His ministry spanned over five decades and reached audiences worldwide through conferences, television, and publications.

I'm not criticizing young preachers, but the truth is, many of them are full of passion yet lack wisdom. Thank God for the older saints who recognize that their calling is to impart wisdom, sound advice, and guidance to the next generation.

No one taught me this—I had to learn the hard way. Still, God's faithfulness has brought us to this point, and the future is as bright as God's promises!

# Chapter Eight

## Collaboration Creates Multiplication

### The Power of Collaboration

God has called us to collaborate because we're stronger united—together, we can do extraordinary things for God. This book really speaks to the heart of Thrive Church's core, but its message is meant for everyone, not just those who call Thrive Church Honesdale home. That's why it's important for everyone to take moments to pause and reflect:

- Where have I come from?
- Where am I going?

The message of this book is bold, challenging, and intentional. It speaks to who we are, both individually and as a community, what we are building, and what God is doing among us.

> "So on October 2 the wall was finished—just fifty-two days after we had begun. When our enemies and the surrounding nations heard about it, they

were frightened and humiliated. They realized this work had been done with the help of our God."

— Nehemiah 6:15-16 (NLT)

This vision came to life through planning, prayer, and persistence.

Our church participated in a community Christmas parade that ended in the city square. It feels like a scene from a Hallmark movie, and it's a great way to connect with the community. So, we came together as a church to build a float on the back of a truck. The night before, a snowstorm hit the area, causing a power outage across the region. I spent most of the night with a young man from our church, plowing snow. Early Saturday morning, we jumped into a truck to clear the church parking lot and walkways. As soon as we started, my phone began to fill up with messages.

*Pastor, I'm sorry—I can't be there. We still don't have power.*

*Pastor, we'd love to help, but we're still without heat.*

I told people, "If you need a shower, we have one in the building next door. We've got heat, and we'll even feed you."

Most of the messages I received were about people who couldn't make it, so I wasn't expecting to find many people when I arrived at the church. When we pulled into the parking lot with the flatbed truck for the float, I was surprised by how many people had already arrived. I walked into the building next to the church, and there were so many ladies working together that I felt like a rooster in a henhouse! They had plans—big ones. And I stood there thinking, 'How are we going to get all this done? This is going to be expensive!'

But thank God for collaboration. Someone spoke up and said, "Hey, we have a little log cabin on our farm. What if we use that instead of building a gingerbread house on the float?" Another idea. Another collaboration. Another solution. One creative-minded lady showed up with more supplies than Heinz has pickles.

## Different Gifts, One Purpose

Everyone has different gifts, but when we come together as the body of Christ, united under God's vision, amazing things happen. I'll be honest, there were so many ladies working on that float that I said, "This rooster is getting out of the henhouse. Y'all have it covered—I'll be next door."

I went to the church for a bit of solitude, or so I thought. I walked in and found more people cleaning and setting up for the next day, joyfully working to prepare God's house. Week after week, they show up. They clean, they worship, and they pray over this place.

I sat down in the media booth and marveled at what I was witnessing. It wasn't that long ago that we didn't have much. We were in that rented building across the street with just a handful of people. Hosting these kinds of events usually meant my wife, a few others, and I would be worn out from doing all the work.

That day was different. People kept showing up unexpectedly.

*Pastor, what can I do?*

*How can I help?*

*I'm here to build a float.*

*I'm here to clean.*

I didn't know where they were coming from—it was incredible. So many people, each using their unique talents and gifts, working together to move forward with what God had called us to do.

## Collaboration Creates Multiplication

If a church wants to grow and fulfill God's calling, collaboration is essential. To go where God has called us and do what He has tasked us with, we must work together.

Not long ago, we were preparing for Thrive's Giving—a Thanksgiving meal we host for the church—and I must admit, we couldn't afford to do it. We called everyone we knew and asked them to make something. Nineteen women stepped up—cooking turkeys, making sides, and bringing everything together.

Now, the Lord has brought us to a place where we can have these meals catered, so everyone can enjoy the experience together without exhausting anyone.

## The Power of Working Together

I look back with gratitude for the many people who willingly came together and worked hard because they saw something greater than themselves and beyond their immediate personal comfort.

*Many hands make the work light.*

As I sat in the media booth that day, watching everything happening before me, I thought about how blessed we were. Forty to fifty people buzzed around the church on a Saturday, doing whatever they could to help—not because they were forced, their arms were twisted, or they felt guilty, but because they were happy to sow into the vision and collaborate.

Imagine what could happen if we:

- Prayed together
- Planned together
- Gave generously together

If we unite in faith and generosity, going above and beyond, how much more could we accomplish? Few things attract God's presence like gratitude, especially when we come together as a church family to glorify Him. That's true collaboration.

## God Has Always Called Us to Collaborate

Collaboration involves working together and cooperating, which I believe has always been God's heart for humanity.

Everything God created, He called good. In the beginning, He made mankind and said, *"This is very good."* But then, God changed the narrative.

He said, *"It is not good for man to be alone."* That's the first time something was deemed not good. This shows that God valued collaboration—right from the beginning. Everything He sees and creates is good. Then He makes man in His image and calls it very good.

And yet, He says: *"You know what's not good? For man to be alone."*

## The Danger of Isolation

The first problem in the Bible isn't sin—it's solitude. Before sin ever appears, God says, *"It's not good for man to be alone."* Sin is a major issue, no doubt. But the initial problem was isolation—living life disconnected from others and not participating in what God is doing.

When we're not engaging in collaboration or working together, we begin to shut down. We start thinking: "I'm just better off by myself." Or "I've been hurt before, so I need to isolate." Isolation goes against what God has called us to do.

God saw that Adam needed a partner—someone to work with, collaborate with, and help fulfill the vision God had for their lives. Even Jesus believed in collaboration so strongly that His last prayer on Earth was for believers to be united—that we would work together, collaborate, and love one another. *"By this, the world will know that you are My disciples—by your love for one another"* (John 13:35).

## The Math of Collaboration

The Bible declares in Deuteronomy 32:30: *"One can put a thousand to flight, but two can put ten thousand."* That math doesn't add up. In God's kingdom, collaboration doesn't just add—it multiplies.

> "Again, truly I tell you, if two of you on earth agree
> about anything they ask for, it will be done for
> them by my Father in heaven. For where two or
> three gather in my name, there am I with them."
>
> — Matthew 18:19-20

So what would God do with all of us if we decided to work together? Collaboration is not just addition—it's multiplication.

Faith Does Not Maintain, It Multiplies

Then God blessed them and said:

"Be fruitful and multiply; fill the earth and subdue it;
have dominion over the fish of the sea, over the
birds of the air, and over every living thing that
moves on the earth."

— Genesis 1:28 (NKJV)

Collaboration has always been part of God's plan. He designed us to work together, build together, and grow together. When we do this, multiplication happens.

In Matthew chapter 25, Jesus tells the parable of the talents (Matthew 25:14-30). Some people are productive with what they are given, while others are not. When the master returns, the man who buried his talent out of fear has it taken from him and given to the one who multiplied what he had. We are called to multiply.

Faith isn't static. If you feel stuck, it's probably because you aren't walking in faith. Faith advances into the future. Still, we must recognize that collaboration results in multiplication.

How will we grow? By working together. How will we achieve this? By coming together.

We wanted to build a float for the Christmas parade. *How's it going to happen?* I didn't know. *What do you know about building floats?* Nothing. I don't know anything about floats. But I had a flatbed truck, so I said, "You can use my truck." I was willing to put it out there, help pay for it, and volunteer my time, talent, and treasure. I don't know anything about designing floats—I'm not artsy, and I don't do crafts. But thank God some people are! Thank God for those who are gifted in the arts. Thank God for the creatives. Because together, we make it happen.

The pastor outlines the vision, but the body of Christ decides how fast we achieve it.

There are people in my church who have a deep understanding of communication media. I know a little, but I support them in every way I can. I collaborate with them because I know God has called us to use media in our ministry.

I don't understand social media; I don't care about it, honestly. Still, I'm grateful for people with a keen eye for it who do incredible work.

We collaborate—maybe it's designing a float or cooking food. Whatever it is, we come together, collaborate, and bring a vision to build something great.

Our kids' ministry is fantastic. I don't know much about kids, except that they like sugar, are expensive, and for some reason, they all seem to like me. I don't always understand children, but I'm grateful for those who do.

I love Nehemiah's story from the Bible because he isn't a pastor, preacher, evangelist, or miracle worker. He's just an ordinary guy—just like you and me.

Nehemiah lived in exile under King Artaxerxes in the Persian Empire. He served as the king's cupbearer—the most dispensable job in history. However, Nehemiah is deeply troubled over Jerusalem's condition when he receives a vision from God through prayer. God gives him a plan to carry out this vision of repairing the walls of Jerusalem, which he then presents to the king while asking for permission to go to Jerusalem.

Very often, God's vision for your life comes from brokenness. Let me ask you—what breaks your heart? What touches your heart is usually connected to your purpose. Nehemiah's heart was broken for Jerusalem, and his goal was to rebuild its walls. Do you know what that involved? A lot of collaboration.

If we collaborate, God will multiply our efforts. Your marriage needs collaboration. Your business needs collaboration.

My brother and I recently had breakfast with a guy who's further along in business than we are. You know what we can do? Collaborate. We can learn some things from him. I told him I wanted to learn what he knew because I wanted to be where he is someday. He was also willing to teach me everything I wanted to know.

Your circle of friends should be a genuine, lively collaboration. From Nehemiah's life, we learn that collaboration needs a few essential elements...

# Chapter Nine

## The Foundation of Collaboration

### Collaboration Requires Clear Conviction

Nehemiah was a man with a vision. When you have a vision, you become a person on a mission. But there's no way to fulfill your mission without conviction in your heart.

> So I arrived in Jerusalem. Three days later, I slipped
> out during the night, taking only a few others
> with me. I had not told anyone about the plans
> God had put in my heart for Jerusalem. We took
> no pack animals with us except the donkey I was
> riding. After dark I went out through the Valley
> Gate, past the Jackal's Well, and over to the Dung
> Gate to inspect the broken walls and burned
> gates.
>
> — Nehemiah 2:11-13 (NLT)

When Nehemiah arrived in Jerusalem, he didn't just show up and announce his plan. Instead, he researched first before taking action. At night, with no one around, he examined the city with a few close friends and started asking some critical questions. *"Okay, God, You gave us this vision. What will this require of us? What's it going to cost? What will it take to rebuild these walls?"*

Nehemiah wasn't in Jerusalem aiming to become a carpenter. He traveled there in obedience to God's call. The fire of conviction inside him drove him to act—to stand up, move forward, and evaluate the situation. He walked through the ruins before talking about rebuilding.

Before you talk it out, you need to walk it out. Many people see themselves as experts with a lot of wisdom to share, but they often don't practice what they preach. You should start by walking it out, not just talking about it. Talk is cheap.

Make a plan. Ask God for a vision by sharing with Him where you want to be in five months, five years, or where you hope your family will be in ten years. Let God give you the vision to fulfill your desires.

I spoke with a businessman recently. He looked my brother and me in the eye and said, "You have two kids, and you have three. Let me tell you the most valuable thing you have: those kids. That's why you're doing all this. I know where your heart is. That's why I want to help." This wasn't even a Christian man.

Collaboration leads to multiplication and fosters a clear conviction—not just about sin (though that's part of it), but also about your calling. You think, *"God, I need to act. I can't keep living day after day, paycheck to paycheck."* Then you feel a strong conviction about what God has called you to do. As you collaborate with others, the vision moves forward. And thank God, people show up—people who know how to build a float. People with ideas. People who know how to get things done.

Do you follow your own advice? What are you actually doing—not just what you're saying? Nehemiah didn't just receive the vision; he took part in it. Jesus never asks you to do something He hasn't already done Himself.

> Then He said to them all, "If anyone desires to come
> after Me, let him deny himself, and take up his
> cross daily, and follow Me."
>
> — Luke 9:23 (NKJV)

When you have a vision of the cross, it brings clear conviction into your life. You'll find it hard to go to a certain club with the cross on your back. You'll struggle to cheat on your wife with the cross on your back. You'll find it difficult to feed an addiction while carrying that cross. Why? Because you're convicted by the vision of what Jesus has done for you, and it changes everything. Are you truly living this out? Are you genuinely putting it into practice in your life?

> "For whoever desires to save his life will lose it, but
> whoever loses his life for My sake will save it. For
> what profit is it to a man if he gains the whole
> world, and is himself destroyed or lost?"
>
> — Luke 9:24-25 (NKJV)

Yes, Jesus calls us to go the extra mile—but it pales in comparison to the fact that He walked through Hell so we might walk into Heaven. There are two crucial things you need on your faith journey: You must *surrender* your life to Jesus and *submit* to the call to serve Him, with a clear conviction in your heart.

Giving money, time, or resources doesn't earn you a place in Heaven. So why do we give? Because we love. I don't give to receive; I give because I love Him. Your generosity helps others find their way to Heaven. It advances the gospel and moves the vision forward. As we sow, a harvest follows, and people come to Christ.

You're blessed to be a blessing. Saved people serve people; that's a conviction. Of course, Jesus receives all the glory; He did the work so that people can be saved. However, He uses people to bring others to Him. You don't serve because you must; you serve because you have the opportunity. Thank God that people are willing to serve in every way. Everybody can do something.

As I look around Thrive Church, I see people like my grandparents helping others by picking up food. I see individuals managing the media outreach, serving meals, and making sure people cross the street safely. These aren't small acts; they are convictions.

I'm reminded of a businessman who faithfully serves our church, helping park cars. He works hard in his business. But do you know what conviction he holds? "Pastor, I'm saved to serve." He doesn't need to do more; he knows who he is and why he's here. "Well, it's just a parking lot." No—it's a conviction. I'm saved to serve.

People who are truly saved serve others. This is a strong belief of mine. I don't need to motivate or coach anyone to do it. If you are genuinely saved, you will naturally want to serve.

I want to fulfill my role. How about you? I trust that God will fulfill His role. He's given me an opportunity to be a blessing—and He's given the same opportunity to you.

Collaboration begins with you. We have a revelation: we're better together. We're built for community.

*I'm looking for a life-giving church.*

Are you a life-giving person? You won't find a life-giving church unless you are one. Otherwise, you'll just drain the life out of everyone else.

*I want encouraging friends.*

Then, be an encouraging person. *"What a man sows, he will also reap"* (Galatians 6:7). It's not just about money—it includes everything. Do you want good leaders? Be a good follower. Do you want a generous community? Sow generous seeds.

Conviction leads to collaboration. Collaboration fosters multiplication. I may lead a church, but I also actively participate in it. I'm not asking people to do anything that my family and I haven't discussed, prayed about, and committed to ourselves.

We've already counted the cost, evaluated the call, and declared, "We're in it to win it." Lord, it's Yours, no matter the cost. We're going to lead the way. Why? Because I believe so deeply in God's vision.

Collaboration creates multiplication.

## Collaboration Requires Compelling Communication

Every God-given vision ultimately turns into a shared one. If your vision is only for yourself, it's not a true God-given vision. We are blessed to be a blessing.

It's crucial to understand and stay sensitive to God's timing on a matter. Yet, there comes a point when you must speak up and share what He's put in your heart. When you do, you also need to realize this: God's vision for your life is never meant to be fulfilled alone. It always requires support from others.

Effective communication fosters healthy relationships, which I often emphasize. We should engage in open, honest, and regular discussions. We can sit down and talk. You can ask me anything, and I hope you allow me to do the same. If there's an issue, we'll work through it together. It's crucial to keep open, free-flowing communication because unresolved conflict can lead to toxic behavior.

Healthy communication is rarely straightforward. Men and women have different ways of communicating. Research shows that the average woman uses about 20,000 words a day, while the average man speaks fewer than 7,000. We communicate differently, but we still need each other.

## Communication Makes Collaboration Work

Collaboration often fails simply because we struggle with communication. Whether in a marriage, a business, a family, or a church—if we don't communicate, collaboration falls apart.

*But the church is growing. That means more chances for things to get complicated.*

Perhaps. However, that's a flimsy excuse to stay stagnant. Effective communication is essential for successful collaboration. We must work to communicate clearly with each other.

## Unity Is the Real Battleground

It won't be some big, blatant sin that destroys the church—not a scandal or public failure. That's not what will bring us down. Jesus said it clearly: *"A house divided against itself will not stand"* (Mark 3:25). That's the real threat.

The Enemy is actively trying to divide the body of Christ and destroy collaboration. However, I also believe that if the church rises up, stays united in faith, and works together, then the Devil knows his days are numbered.

*"I believe differently from the people at that church, so I could never go there or receive anything from them."*

Don't hesitate to work together. I've partnered with people from many different backgrounds—Word of Faith, Presbyterian, and everything in between—because at the core, it's about Jesus. If we agree on the essentials—Christ, the cross, and the resurrection—we can collaborate to achieve God's vision. However, if you're unwilling to collaborate, you will never fulfill what God has called you to do.

## Collaboration Requires Conflict Resolution

God wants us to live in community. However, the bigger the community, the higher the chance of hurt, offense, and disappointment. Living in a community means conflicts will happen. Sadly, many people never resolve these conflicts because they think they are better off alone.

The blessing of community far exceeds its burdens. If you let it, there's potential for offense every day.

The Devil sows seeds of division, seeking to isolate people and ultimately destroy them. He puts ideas in your mind that were never spoken and makes you believe they were.

I once had a young man come to me and say, "You were preaching about me last night. I know you were talking about me." He was angry. Then his parents got involved, and all these people started yelling at me. I told them, "I promise you, with everything I have, I wasn't thinking about you." The truth is, I wasn't even talking about a guy—I was referring to an entirely different situation.

That's how the Devil operates. He whispers things like: *They don't like you,* or *Remember what happened?* Don't take the bait—forget it. God forgot it, so you should too. God casts our sins into the sea of forgetfulness. The sins you can't forget, God can't even remember.

## Unresolved Conflict Destroys Collaboration

I appreciate open and honest conversations. I have no problem with conflict; what really bothers me is unresolved conflict.

All it takes is a conversation. Still, people often hold onto offenses for years. Unresolved conflict inevitably becomes toxic, hindering collaboration and multiplication.

When Nehemiah arrived in Jerusalem, he discovered that external threats didn't cause the greatest turmoil—they stemmed from within.

> "When I heard their outcry and these charges, I was
> very angry. I pondered them in my mind and then
> accused the nobles and officials. I told them, 'You
> are charging your own people interest!' So I called
> together a large meeting to deal with them."

> — Nehemiah 5:6-7

Conflict isn't inherently bad, but unresolved conflict definitely is. Resolved conflict builds you up, while unresolved conflict turns into toxic poison, the bait of Satan.

Unresolved conflict and the offense it causes weaken collaboration. We must be individuals who choose forgiveness, willingly live without offense, and do everything possible to foster collaboration. Life is too short to be consumed by hurt, offense, or bitterness.

Unresolved conflict infiltrates every part of your life. People tend to hold onto offenses, but the more you suppress your feelings, the more they spill over into your marriage, family, and church community.

*You don't know what they did to me.* I'm sorry that happened, but you can't live there.

*"Yea, though I walk through the valley of the shadow of death..."* (Psalm 23:4 KJV). He didn't say to set up camp there. You're meant to walk through it—keep moving. Don't settle into your hurt.

Unforgiveness is like drinking poison while expecting the other person to die. You are called to multiply, but to do so, you must collaborate; you cannot collaborate with someone you resent.

## Jesus Restores Our Ability to Collaborate

Jesus didn't die just to save us from sin and get us to Heaven. His death restored our ability to collaborate with God and each other. From the very beginning, God's desire has been for collaboration. Sin broke that connection, but at the cross, Jesus restored it.

This has been God's heartbeat for the church since Genesis 1. However, instead of the church multiplying and fulfilling what God has called us to do, people choose to live with offense, which harms the church.

Don't let offense ruin your collaboration. It's time to mature—be accountable—and accept responsibility. Collaboration matters more than your offense.

## Nehemiah's Example: Rebuilding Through Collaboration

> "So on October 2 the wall was finished—just fifty-
> two days after we had begun. When our enemies
> and the surrounding nations heard about it, they
> were frightened and humiliated. They realized this
> work had been done with the help of our God."

> — Nehemiah 6:15-16 (NLT)

*How did they rebuild the wall?* They collaborated, and God helped them.

*How did your business succeed?* With the help of our God.

*How did your family survive?* With the help of our God.

My prayer is that people will look at Thrive Church and see that this work was accomplished with the help of our God.

## Protecting Unity

Collaboration requires conflict resolution. We must strive to maintain our unity. We need to work diligently to reduce distractions, both inside and outside the home. This is not something I take lightly. People's souls are at stake. If you understand this revelation, it will inspire you to live your life with purpose and intention.

Collaboration needs conflict resolution. We must protect this collaboration because the world is watching. When they see a church that is unified and working together, they will say, "Look what God has done."

# Chapter Ten

## Principles of Compelling Communication

But now I said to them, "You know very well what
trouble we are in. Jerusalem lies in ruins, and its
gates have been destroyed by fire. Let us rebuild
the wall of Jerusalem and end this disgrace!" Then
I told them about how the gracious hand of God
had been on me, and about my conversation with
the king.

— Nehemiah 2:17-18 (NLT)

### Point Out the Problem

I have no issue with people pointing out problems—if they also
bring a solution.

God-given visions will awaken you from apathy. There is danger in
isolating your life for comfort and shutting out everyone's voice.
When no one can point out the problems or threats facing you,
what happens by default? You settle for less than God's best. Why?

Because you've become comfortable with your situation. You start to accept things that are less than God's best for you because you're unwilling to take advice.

Nehemiah highlights the problem—Jerusalem is in ruins. The walls are broken down, and the gates are burned. However, this isn't news to the people still living in Jerusalem. They've grown accustomed to it. Day after day, they walk over the fallen walls and pass by the charred gates. Instead of coming up with a plan to fix the walls, they've learned to live with it and accept it as normal.

Without a God-given vision and people to identify these problems, you might find yourself tolerating rubble in your life. Are you so comfortable that you think, *I know it all. I've got it all together. Who are you to tell me anything?* Maybe God wants to work through someone else to help you. If you're not careful, you might accept ongoing dysfunction. It's easy to ignore addiction and endure brokenness.

Here's how this can play out in your life: You accept constant dysfunction by saying things like, *That's just my family.* But what you need to say is: *Hey, let's rebuild this. Let's fix this mess.* You must be willing to grow, identify problems, and—most importantly—bring solutions. When we work together, things can improve.

*But I come from a dysfunctional family.*

That doesn't mean you have to continue the pattern. I hear people say all the time, *Pastor, it runs in my family.* I tell them, *Let it run out. It ended when the blood of Jesus covered you. My friend, you're called to more.*

You can't change what you tolerate. You need to reach a point where the problem bothers you enough to jolt you awake. You get what you allow.

Effective communication isn't just about pointing out problems, even though some believe that's their spiritual gift. I grew up in church and have met people who often say, *Well, there's a problem over here, and there's another problem over there.* There are nine spiritual gifts and nine fruits of the Spirit. However, you won't find among them the gift of pointing out problems!

We recently held a baptismal service and celebration. The food was excellent, the service was outstanding, people got baptized, my dad led the worship, and I preached. Everything went smoothly. However, as soon as the service ended, I met with a few team members. I said, "Here's what we need to change. Here's how we can improve. Here's how we can get better." I didn't say it negatively; it's about striving for a spirit of excellence. I don't become comfortable with the status quo because comfort and familiarity are the enemies of growth.

Our weekly Sunday 6:30 PM service grew so much that eventually we couldn't fit everyone. We added an extra service at 4:30 PM, which is now fully booked. These are good problems to have.

Is it comfortable doing two services? Not really. Is it easy? No. I'm exhausted when I wake up for work in the morning. However, here's the thing: it's worth it because we're stepping outside our comfort zone by collaborating and constantly trying to improve. I'll share with our team areas where I want to grow, but I'm not just pointing out the problems; I'm also offering solutions.

Effective communication doesn't just highlight problems; it also presents solutions. When Nehemiah pointed out the rubble, he didn't stop there. He said, "Let us rebuild the wall of Jerusalem and end this disgrace!" He identified the problem but then pointed to the solution. Similarly, we need to be people who not only recognize issues but also offer practical, faith-filled solutions. When God gives a vision, He also provides a plan—and He expects us to walk it out in faith.

If you want to collaborate and multiply what God has placed in your heart, you can't just point out problems; you need to become a problem solver. When you do, you'll find that collaboration naturally leads to multiplication.

## Describe the Solution

If your vision doesn't address a problem, what's the point? God is a God of multiplication. He moves us from strength to strength, glory to glory, victory to victory, and faith to faith.

When we collaborate, things multiply. I have a team of people who understand the ins and outs of various media communications. I don't fully grasp all of it, but I do have a vision. I say, "I've got a vision to create podcasts, stream services, and build an online presence. What's the plan? How are we going to make it happen? What's it going to cost? How do we get our ducks in a row so that when the blessing of God comes, we're ready to run with the vision and fulfill what God has called us to do?" But I can't do this alone. Thank God for the people willing to collaborate to fulfill God's vision.

If you have a vision from God, it will resolve a problem—whether spiritual, physical, financial, relational, or emotional. A vision from God confronts problems.

Nehemiah faced a serious problem: the place was in ruins, the walls were destroyed, the gates were burned, and the people lived among rubble. However, a God-given vision doesn't just identify the problem—it also provides a solution. It instills a burden and passion in people to make a change, rebuild the walls, and inspire their imagination—not of what is, but of what could be.

## God-Given Vision Appeals to the Imagination

We started Thrive Church at the end of 2020. A young woman attended our first service on December 23, 2020 —when the world was shut down. A mother of five was gloriously delivered from a significant addiction and the lifestyle that went with it during that first service. My heart broke for her. We launched with a preview service, but after hearing her testimony, we knew we had to establish a church.

We didn't have a congregation at that time. We didn't have much money. We didn't have much of anything. But we had a vision. We carried a burden and a passion from God. I said, *God, I believe we can do this. I believe You've called us. If it's Your will, it's Your bill. I trust You'll provide the people and the resources. We're going to work as if everything depends on us and pray as if everything depends on You. Somewhere in the middle, we're going to meet God, because I believe You've given us a vision, and You will enable the collaboration to happen.* And what did God do? The same thing He did for Nehemiah. He began to appeal to people's imaginations.

## Imagination Is One of God's Most Powerful Tools

Which direction does your imagination tend to go? Does it lean toward fear, or does it move toward faith? Does it focus on problems, or does it guide you to solutions?

> Now to Him who is able to do exceedingly abundantly above all that we ask or think, according to the power that works in us.
>
> — Ephesians 3:20 (NKJV)

If you can dream it, God can do it.

For years, I drove past the building where our church now meets. It was rundown and falling apart—a true eyesore. I thought, 'That place is an embarrassment.' I knew we needed a new location, but I couldn't imagine God wanting us in such a run-down place. That's not the God I serve. I believe God operates with a spirit of excellence and wants us to represent Him well. I remember thinking, 'God, You're better than that. Is that really the best we can do?' God had given me a burden, but I didn't understand it at first.

## A Burden That Wouldn't Let Me Go

One day, I rode past the building on my motorcycle when the power of God came over me. At that time, we were preparing to move to South Florida. We had everything organized. God had been good to us, and we were blessed. Everything was in place.

But as I drove past the building that day, the Lord placed something on my heart. I felt like Jonah, except there aren't any whales in Honesdale. However, I knew where God was calling me to go. Like Jonah, I offered every excuse I could think of: *God, it's 2020. The world is shut down. We don't have a congregation. We don't have money. We don't have people. We're selling what we do have and moving to where we want to go. I want to live in sunshine!*

But God placed a burden and a passion in my heart.

I've told you before: The things that irritate you or rub you the wrong way often indicate what God wants to use you to change. I could have made excuses; that would have been easy. But God gave us a passion, a burden, and a vision. He provided us with a plan. And then He gave us what I call collaboration.

## Collaboration Produces Multiplication

During 2020, when the world was shut down, God started bringing people together. I began meeting contractors, painters, plumbers, and other skilled workers who, despite having no work, were willing to help move the vision forward. I had no idea how it was all going to happen. I spent many nights in that building praying. We started from humble beginnings and eventually leased the former Presbyterian church down by the park as a temporary meeting location. We didn't have the money to do that—but we did it anyway.

## It's Not Always Easy

The money didn't come in from church offerings, so Carolyn and I did whatever we had to do. We paid the rent and utilities, doing whatever it took because I knew God had called us and given us a vision, a plan, and a burden. It wasn't always easy or comfortable but in every difficulty, He made it happen. Every challenge poses an opportunity—you can either rise above it or wallow in it. You can choose to be a victim, or you can be a victor.

We come alongside people, guiding them toward the hope we have in Jesus Christ. A God-given solution can turn a nightmare into a God-inspired dream, and that's exactly what we do—one step at a time.

## Compelling Communication Reinforces the Reason

Nehemiah recognized the problem: Jerusalem's people were vulnerable, but he now posed an important question—how much longer would they accept this shame? He approached the people and asked, *How much longer will we live like this? How much longer will this situation stay the same? We're better than this. We're God's children.*

What Nehemiah did was powerful—he appealed to their pride and identity. He reminded them:

- We are better together.
- We have the hope of glory living inside us.
- We can do better.
- Surely, we can strive for excellence.
- Surely, we will not remain in this muck.

*We've already settled for too long. We've lived in the rubble. But it's time to get up and move forward,* Nehemiah told the people.

The Bible says, *"The righteous may fall seven times, but they get up again"* (Proverbs 24:16). And that's what Nehemiah was calling them to do—to rise up again, keep climbing, keep fighting, and keep believing.

*God, I believe You gave me this vision,* Nehemiah must have prayed. *God, I believe we're going to accomplish this thing. How is it going to happen? I don't know. But it's up to You.*

But Nehemiah didn't stop there. He wasn't just relying on God; he was committed to working as if everything depended on him and praying as if everything depended on God. Along the way, collaboration would bring the vision to life.

## We are God's People

Nehemiah reminded them of the promise they had had from the beginning. However, due to their rebellion, sin, and disobedience, they found themselves in this situation. It was time to awaken and shake off the disgrace.

*I want to remind you,* Nehemiah might have said, *We are the children of God.*

Today, I want to remind you that we are children of God. I'm appealing to our identity in Christ Jesus, our Lord.

## Communication Clarifies the Urgency

*Why should we start now? Look at this mess, Nehemiah.* The people of Nehemiah's day said that to him, and people have said the same to me about my church.

*It's 2020. Don't you know that the world has shut down?*

*Why don't you wait until next year? Why don't you wait five years?*

*Why don't you wait for a different president?*

*Why don't you wait for a different job?*

*Why don't you wait for the economy to change?*

My answer was always the same: *There's no better time than now because God said to do it now.* Anyone can make excuses. I don't want to wait. Now is the time. The Bible states, *Now to Him who is able* (Ephesians 3:20). Now is the season. Now is the time to collaborate and declare: "We're moving forward with this thing in Jesus' name."

## God's Favor Demands Action

Nehemiah clarifies it with urgency. He says, *I will tell you why the time is right now—because God's hand is upon me and because the king has given me favor.* Now is our time to step out in faith, launch out, and believe God for His best and move forward with this vision. Not tomorrow. Not next month, next year, or five years from now. Now is the time. We've got urgency. We've prayed and planned, and now is the time. Let's do it while we have God's hand upon us. Let's move forward while we have God's favor with us.

## Excuses Kill Vision

The king of Persia provided Nehemiah with the resources to travel to Jerusalem. Nehemiah is believed to have been enslaved under King Artaxerxes. He is the cupbearer, at the bottom of the totem pole—he is beneath the pole.

*Well, God, my situation is different.* No, you're making excuses. You're being lazy.

*Yeah, but God, I don't have the money.* That's not what He asked.

*God, I don't have the promise.* That's not what He said.

The Bible says, *Now to Him who is able.* Stop making excuses and telling God what you cannot do when He is the one who said you can do it. You can do all things through Christ who strengthens you (Philippians 4:13). All things.

I don't hang around with people who tell me what I can't do. I prefer people who tell me what I can do.

How will it happen? It will happen through collaboration—collaboration with God and with each other. It will happen through our diverse gifts. We work together with one mind, one spirit, and a unified body of Christ, and we can accomplish everything God has called us to do.

# Chapter Eleven

## The Bigger the Vision, the Greater the Opposition

### God Gives the 'What' Before the 'How'

God always gives you the what before He shows you the how. He provides a vision for the future and then calls you to step out in faith. As you do, He begins to reveal the plan for how you're going to accomplish it.

> Sanballat was very angry when he learned that we
> were rebuilding the wall. He flew into a rage and
> mocked the Jews, saying in front of his friends and
> the Samarian army officers, "What does this
> bunch of poor, feeble Jews think they're doing?
> Do they think they can build the wall in a single
> day by just offering a few sacrifices? Do they actu-
> ally think they can make something of stones
> from a rubbish heap—and charred ones at that?"

Tobiah the Ammonite, who was standing beside him, remarked, "That stone wall would collapse if even a fox walked along the top of it!"

— Nehemiah 4:1-3 (NLT)

God always calls us to step out of our comfort zone, to step out of the boat. The problem with staying in the boat is that you only ever meet disciples. But when you step out of the boat and begin to walk on water, you meet Jesus every time. Sometimes, the wind blows, and the waves crash—but when you step out in faith, you are walking with Jesus.

Sometimes, stepping out in faith means leaving the boat of religion, where all the disciples are—and that's fine—but I don't want just to be where the disciples are. I want to be where *Jesus* is. I want to take that step of faith and step out on top of the water, saying, "As long as I keep my eyes on You, my vision is fixed." I want to walk on the water where Jesus is.

I don't want just to meet disciples. I want to reach people far from God. I want to see churches filled with God's people—and, closer to home, I want to reach my community and live beyond myself, saying, "We're in this city for this city, and we're going to do something great by God's grace."

## God Gives the 'What' Before the 'How'

The "what" is the vision; the "how" is the plan. Many people get caught up in the details, which stops them from stepping out in faith. I've decided to trust Jesus with the how.

*I don't believe they'll ever be able to do something like that.*

Thankfully, we're not dependent on you. We're relying on Him—on His power working within us. I'm not concerned with someone's "How are you going to do that?" I'm focused on what He has called us to do.

I believe God is fully able. In fact, I'm completely convinced. I don't care who criticizes, mocks, or says a fox could run across it and knock it down. We're going to build this thing by God's grace. We're going to follow the Holy Spirit's guidance and step out once more. God has been faithful to us in building our church over the last four years, and He will remain faithful to what He's called you to do as well.

## Commitment Precedes Provision

With God, commitment precedes provision. In the natural world, people say, *Well, I've got X amount of dollars, so I can do X, Y, and Z.* But when God calls you to step out, He provides the what—and then requests your commitment. That commitment always comes first. I wish it worked the other way around, but that wouldn't require faith. Faith calls us to step into the unknown. And when we do, He is faithful to provide what we need.

There have been many times when our church has given entire offerings to other ministries. *How are you going to pay the bills?* He'll take care of it. *Well, that's crazy.* That's how faith works. We're following the guidance of the Holy Spirit. God says, *Sow the seed, go for the goal.* We must be willing and obedient to what He has called us to do.

Provision always follows vision. As we step out in faith with the what, God always provides the *how.* I don't know about you, but I'm grateful for that. When God speaks to you to do something, your response isn't to question it; your response is to obey it.

## Seed Makes Way for Harvest

In October, we celebrate Pastor Appreciation. I'm grateful for such a generous church. However, this past year, we sowed the entire appreciation offering to Samaritan's Purse to help with hurricane relief. During the second week, we also contributed the offering to Tony Suárez, founder of Revivalmakers.

My seed makes way for my harvest. What I make happen for others, God will make happen for us. I know in whom I have believed. What I do for God's house, God will do for my house.

*Well, you gave it away.* It doesn't matter. He'll bring it back—some thirty, some sixty, some hundredfold.

It's more than just money; it touches every part of life. When you give generously, generosity returns. When you give love, love comes back.

## Expect Criticism When You Step Out

The only people who don't face criticism are those who aren't doing anything. Success naturally draws criticism. Have you ever heard people criticize homeless folks? No. Do you know who gets criticized? People who put themselves out there and pursue their vision.

The bigger the vision, the more opposition you'll face. I'm here to share the Word of God. You must understand that when God gives you a vision, develops a plan to achieve it, and brings people together to work toward it, opposition is inevitable.

The greater the blessing, the greater the attack. You have preachers running around as if there's no opposition in this world. They are being dishonest because they are preaching something that the Word of God does not teach.

Every man or woman in Scripture who received a vision from God faced opposition. It is scriptural to be challenged; however, it is also unscriptural to be defeated.

We live in a broken world filled with broken people. Challenges will come. Yes, God has His people—though so does the Devil. And remember: when Lucifer was cast out of Heaven, a third of the angels were cast out with him. Where do you think they went?

Resistance develops strength. When you face resistance, it's usually an indication that you're heading in the right direction.

I believe that criticism plants seeds of division. People might try to halt your momentum or break up your team, but if God has called you to move forward, no one can stop you.

## Vision Brings Change—and Change Brings Criticism

Vision drives change. It ventures into the unknown, which involves stepping into what you can't control. When people lose control, they often criticize.

Criticism doesn't only come from others—it often starts from within. Sometimes, the loudest voices of doubt and unbelief come from within the camp.

Consider Jesus in Mark 5. Jairus walks with Jesus back to his house. But then comes the bad news: *Why bother the teacher anymore? Your daughter's not sleeping—she's dead* (Mark 5:35).

The Bible says that Jesus overheard what they said. Why? Because on the journey of faith, there will always be critics—people who tell you what you cannot do.

## Don't Listen to People—Listen to God

I've learned not to listen to people—listen to God instead. I'm not concerned about who tells me what I can't do. I want to be around people who tell me what I can do.

The Word says, *"I can do all things through Christ who strengthens me"* (Philippians 4:13 NKJV). Don't tell me what I can't do.

Maybe it's just my personality, but every time someone tells me I can't do something, I go out and do it twice—once for the Devil and once for them.

*Oh, you can't.* Yes, I can—and I *will*. And then I will do it again, to prove that with God, all things are possible for those who believe.

Even if you're living in exile in Persia or if you're a slave under King Artaxerxes, if you have a vision from God, go to Him in prayer, receive a plan from Him, and gather people to collaborate, then you can build it. You can reach it. You can complete it. You can create something lasting, to the glory of God in Jesus' name.

# Chapter Twelve

## When Opposition Comes, We Must First Go to Prayer

Hear us, our God, for we are despised. Turn their insults back on their own heads. Give them over as plunder in a land of captivity. Do not cover up their guilt or blot out their sins from your sight, for they have thrown insults in the face of the builders.

— Nehemiah 4:4-5

### When Opposition Comes, We Must First Go to Prayer

Nehemiah doesn't talk to his critics; he talks to God. When you pray to God, you can be completely yourself. You can be real and honest with God. He's a mighty God—He can handle it.

*I need to get myself together and come to God.* Just come to Him as you are. He already knows.

*I'm angry. I can't turn to God right now.* He can handle your anger; He's a big God.

Do you remember Peter? He denied Christ three times. He didn't just deny Him—he even swore about it. You can read about it in the Bible (John 18:15-27). What does Jesus do? He prepares a fish breakfast on the beach for Peter (John 21:1-14). Jesus calls Peter back to Himself.

God isn't looking for the perfect version of you. He already knows who you are and understands your deepest thoughts. So why not come to Him and say, "God, I feel upset. God, I feel frustrated. God, I feel hurt. God, this is really affecting me." Be honest and open with Him.

Many people avoid coming to God because they fear being honest with Him. But the truth is, God desires the authentic you, not a mask. He doesn't want the insincere or hidden version of you. He wants the real you—your true heart, habits, and struggles—to come to Him and say, "God, I need You."

Nehemiah turns to God because prayer should be our first response, not our last resort. You should pray to God as soon as opposition begins to threaten you.

## Keep Your Mouth Shut

A few years ago, I faced some of the most intense opposition I've ever encountered while building our church. I went to the Lord, hoping He would send an angel to deal with some people. I wanted to justify myself—because, let's be honest, we all want to justify ourselves when we're under attack.

The Lord said to me, *Keep your mouth shut.* That was the hardest thing He had ever asked me to do. You might think that keeping quiet would be easy. However, I would have preferred to give everything away rather than keep my mouth shut. I wanted to tell my side, but instead, I had to stand there in silence. It was the most difficult thing God ever asked me to do. But having done all to stand—stand firm (Ephesians 6:10-18).

There will always be opposition and critical people. However, the greater the attack, the greater the blessing. We don't get lost in the *how*—we stay focused on the *what*. But we must go to God in prayer first.

## Prayer Realigns Our Focus

My grandfather gave me some brilliant advice that I like to share with people facing tense moments: Whatever the issue is, take a 3 day pause, give yourself some space, and pray.

Most people can't even remember what they were angry about after three days. It's amazing what praying about something over three days can do. It works because prayer shifts our focus. Distraction delays growth, but prayer restores focus.

I heard an incredible testimony from a man in our church, and I love sharing it. He started making knives. These aren't just ordinary knives; they are some of the finest I've ever seen.

He came to me one day and said, "Pastor, I've been praying about what God would have me do concerning giving to the church. Things are tough right now, but I've been praying and I have a plan."

He was using prayer to realign his focus. Then he shifted from praying to planning. He told me, "God told me to sell knives at a craft event—and all the money would go to the church on Vision Sunday."

After the event, I asked him how it went. He sold seven knives. It's funny how God favors the number seven.

Someone else might have said, *I don't have the money, so I can't partici-pate. I have a million excuses for why I can't participate.* But instead, he said, "No. I'm going to pray. I'm going to plan. And I'm going to step into this."

Prayer gets your heart into it. Your soul into it. Your spirit into it.

## Working Hard vs. Working Heart

> So we rebuilt the wall till all of it reached half its
> height, for the people worked with all their heart.
>
> — Nehemiah 4:6

They didn't just work hard—they worked wholeheartedly. Prayer involves your heart when you ask God what He wants you to do.

You might pray something like, *God, I realize that if we collaborate together, even though the economy looks tough and there's opposition, I know together we can build something that's going to last.*

Vision without prayer leads to hard work. Vision combined with prayer motivates you to work wholeheartedly.

I believe we should work hard. I believe God blesses the work of our hands. However, there's a difference between working foolishly and working with all your heart.

Passion motivates you to take actions you wouldn't normally consider. It pushes you past your comfort zone, out of the boat, and into deeper waters.

*God, it looks like hard work—but if I work with all my heart, keep my prayer life focused, and keep my eyes aligned with Your vision, I know—no matter what opposition I face—I'm going to make it, in Jesus' name.*

## Prayer Before Panic

When opposition enters your heart, you need something deep inside that urges you not to give up. When you focus on God's vision, you stand your ground firmly.

Most people, when confronting opposition, see only that. Have you ever met someone like this? All they talk about is their problem. Why? Because they are fixated on the opposition.

You can turn to God, be honest with Him in prayer, and say, *God, I'm coming to You first. Not social media, not my friends, not anything else. I'm coming to You, Lord, first and foremost. God, I'm really upset right here.*

Consider Nehemiah's prayer. He wasn't saying, *Oh God, what a beautiful day today.* No—look at what he prays: *God, I pray You turn it on their heads. God, I pray You scatter my enemies. God, don't even forgive their sins* (Nehemiah 4:4-5). Nehemiah is angry. And guess what? God can handle your anger. So go to Him before telling everyone around you.

*I'm angry.* Then go to God with it.

Jesus had emotions, too. He was in the temple when he saw the money changers and became very angry. This is my favorite version of Jesus. He's fashioning a whip—just staring at them. *I'm about to crack your butts with this thing.* Read it for yourself (John 2:14-16). Jesus flips tables and starts whipping people. He experienced righteous anger. God can handle you at your worst as well as at your best. He is God.

Most people, when faced with opposition, react with panic. However, we serve a God who is greater than any opposition, problem, or storm.

## My God Is So Big, So Strong, and So Mighty

One night, my kids were singing, "My God is so big, so strong, and so mighty. There's nothing my God cannot do."

They were dancing around the house, singing it. I thought about just letting them preach on Sunday night. Because if the people in the seats would catch that message—"My God is so big, so strong, and so mighty, there's nothing my God cannot do"—most of their problems would disappear because their faith would lift them above their issues.

No matter what opposition comes against me, I'm going to make it in Jesus' name because I go to Him in prayer first. I serve a big, strong, and mighty God!

## Stop Complaining About What You Prayed For

Are you complaining about something you prayed for?

Perhaps you prayed for your partner, saying, *God, I just want to be married. Jesus, send me the man of my dreams, my knight in shining armor.*

Six months into the marriage, your knight is snoring on the couch, and now, he's your nightmare. Now, you're complaining about the very thing you prayed for. You prayed for that job, crying out, *God, I just need provision. Please open a door.* But now you're saying, *God, I hate this place,* even though, a little while ago, you didn't have a job.

You insult God, who gave you exactly what you asked for, when you complain about what you prayed for. You prayed for your children. You prayed that God would give you an opportunity. You prayed for a chance to serve. So why are you complaining?

Why is it easier to focus on what we can't do when God has already declared that you can do all things through Christ? I've mentioned before that it's not about equal amounts—it's about equal sacrifice. It's about humbling yourself before God and saying, *Lord, I'm going to pray about my part. I'm going to plan for my part. And I believe that if we collaborate together, even in the face of opposition, we can build something that will last—in Jesus' name.*

## Do You Fold When You Face Resistance?

Does the first sign of opposition make you want to quit? I love passionate people. But sometimes, those same passionate individuals are the first to fold when adversity shows up.

Do you say, *Oh, I just want to quit. I can't do this anymore. I quit. I'm done,* or do you stand your ground? *God, I'm not quitting. I'm going to keep my eyes fixed on You—the Author and Finisher of my faith.*

> They were all trying to frighten us, thinking, "Their hands will get too weak for the work, and it will not be completed." But I prayed, "Now strengthen my hands."
>
> — NEHEMIAH 6:9

## Surround Yourself with People Who Strengthen You

Most people spend more time worrying about who criticizes them than remembering who called them. You should surround yourself with people who support your vision, not weaken it.

Can you imagine a church where people genuinely love spending time together? Where people are excited to serve? Where they show up and say, "How can I help build this?" That's what happens when people are willing to collaborate. That's the kind of church we're building. Be someone who strengthens the vision, not someone who tears it down. Be a person who goes to prayer first, not to panic. Be the individual who remembers that God provides the 'what' before the 'how'—and the 'how' is discovered in prayer.

# Chapter Thirteen

## When Opposition Comes, We Must Pivot

### Battle-Ready Builders

When Nehemiah faced threats and criticism, he didn't give up on building the wall. Instead, he changed his approach to how they were building it.

> From that day on, half of my men did the work, while the other half were equipped with spears, shields, bows and armor. The officers posted themselves behind all the people of Judah who were building the wall. Those who carried materials did their work with one hand and held a weapon in the other, and each of the builders wore his sword at his side as he worked. But the man who sounded the trumpet stayed with me.
>
> — Nehemiah 4:16-18

As we keep building Thrive Church in Honesdale, we're approaching things differently than most church startups. We are not changing the what—we are simply changing the how.

Nehemiah's men were prepared for battle, but they were also ready to build. They didn't give up; they pivoted. That's something I love about Thrive Church—we're always prepared to build, but we're also always ready to fight; fight for the vision and for the souls of people. No opposition will stop us. I've got a Milwaukee hammer drill in one hand and a Browning rifle in the other. A pivot simply means a change in strategy—not a change in vision.

In basketball, a pivot foot is what you use when you run out of your dribble. It's the last offensive move you can make. However, as you pivot, you might spot another opening. The vision isn't finished—the plan has evolved.

I hear pastors say, *I can't figure it out. We've been doing the same thing we've always done, but it just doesn't seem to work anymore.* Well, maybe it's time to pivot.

Some business owners say, *My business was doing great, but since 2020, everything's changed.* Perhaps it's time to think differently. It's time to pivot.

## See Obstacles as Opportunities

When we started streaming on TikTok, some people said, *You can't do that. You need 1,000 followers.* My reply was, *So what?* We posted content, and in the first week, we received several thousand views.

*You should see how bad the comments are. Someone mentioned that you have a butch haircut.* I don't know who Butch is, but apparently, he has great hair.

*They're saying negative things! Good. That means they're watching and listening. And guess what? Our TikTok has grown to over 20,000 subscribers—people we never would have reached otherwise.*

You can let people's comments discourage you and bring you down, or you can let them show that you're making progress by turning obstacles into opportunities. Most people give up on the "what" (the vision) when the "how" (the method) gets tough.

## You'll Lose What You Don't Fight For

*I need to change my spouse.* Perhaps you just need a new approach.

*She doesn't love me like she used to.* Then restoke the fire. Love again. Serve again. Speak life again. Is it *really* easier to find someone else? It's easy to get distracted and lose everything you have.

These days, it's too easy to walk away—too easy to swipe right and start fresh. You risk losing what God gave you if you're not willing to fight for it.

When you're creating a vision—whether it's for marriage, ministry, or business—it takes two essentials: tools to build and weapons to fight.

## Faith Builds and Battles

One evening, I was getting ready to go hunting early the next morning. I had guns spread across the bed and leaned against the dresser while I prepared them for the next day.

Levi, our all-American boy who was supposed to be in bed, joined me and said, "Dad, this is awesome!"

"You're right, buddy. It is pretty awesome."

When Carolyn came upstairs to herd Levi back to bed, she glanced at the guns scattered about and asked, "How many guns do you have?"

I looked into her loving eyes and said with a smile, "Carolyn, Nehemiah said, *'Those who carried materials did their work with one hand and held a weapon in the other'* (Nehemiah 4:17). It takes Milwaukee tools in one hand and Browning guns in the other. I'm just trying to be a biblical man."

Faith requires both. You build with one hand, and you do battle with the other.

Do you want to build a marriage? Fight for it.

Do you want to build a family? Fight for it.

Do you want to build a healthy life? Fight for it.

Do you want to build a business? Fight for it.

Faced with opposition, you don't back down—you keep building while remaining ready to fight.

## God's Divine Pivot

We won't quit; we're simply going to pivot. And you know what? God pivoted for us. He created us to walk with Him in the garden. However, sin ruined the plan. So what did He do? He pivoted. He sent His only Son to take our place. Where Adam failed, Jesus succeeded.

But God didn't discard the vision—He changed His strategy. He said, *I'll sow a seed named Jesus, and I'll reap a harvest of sons and daughters.* God's pivot became our salvation. He did it for you. He did it for me.

# Chapter Fourteen

## When Opposition Comes, We Must Remember

W hen opposition comes—and it will definitely come—first, we turn to prayer; second, we seek a plan from God to adapt; and third, as opposition arises, we must remember.

> After I looked things over, I stood up and said to the
> nobles, the officials and the rest of the people,
> "Don't be afraid of them. Remember the Lord,
> who is great and awesome, and fight for your
> families, your sons and your daughters, your
> wives and your homes."
>
> — Nehemiah 4:14

## Where Are the Men?

I want to address men for a moment. It's time for men to be men again. I'm not putting down women—thank God for them. I'm speaking to men about growing a backbone. It's time to lead your families again and bring them to church.

*I'd like to go tonight, but football is on.* Football can't save your soul. Football can't change your family. Football can't redeem your marriage. Football can't do anything for you.

I like football too—but guess what? These days, you can watch the game later. Why not go to church? Why not take the lead?

We need pulpits that challenge men to become men again. I recently attended a church where the service was great—lots of different people were there. But do you want to know what bothered me? It takes a lot to make me uncomfortable, but on the platform, not a single man was present. In the media booth? Not one man. Ushers, greeters, security—still no men. It was a wonderful service, but I couldn't help thinking: 'Where are the men?'

Bring your family to church again. Pray for your kids. Read the Bible to your kids, serve, and stay committed to your church. Be a man. Be the priest of your house—the man God has called you to be. Don't be a limp-wristed sissy—be a man of God.

You wonder why your kids aren't growing up serving God. Maybe it's because you're not living up to the man God has called you to be.


## Fight for Your Families

Here's what Nehemiah says: *"Remember the Lord, who is great and awesome, and fight for your families, your sons and your daughters, your wives and your homes"* (Nehemiah 4:14). Weapon in one hand, hammer in the other. Sometimes, you must fight for your family, your marriage, and your business. It's time to regain your fighting spirit. This country was founded by people willing to fight.

*They're going to tax us.* Dump the tea! You know your history.

But think of how people react today... *They're going to raise the taxes. Okay—whatever you say.* Come on! Where's your fight?

I love this country. I don't want it to go to Hell. I want it to be the most blessed nation on Earth. How's that going to happen? By returning Jesus to the places where we cast Him out. By standing up and saying, "No—we want God in our schools again. God in our government again. And we're not going to tolerate this garbage."

Imagine if the Church found its voice again—if politicians admitted, *We'd better listen to them because they're a force to be reckoned with.*


## Remember What God Has Done

Vision is about the future, but the fuel for our future comes from God's faithfulness in the past.

Nehemiah didn't go to Jerusalem just to repair the walls—he went to rebuild them. There's a big difference. More importantly, he aimed to restore the souls of broken people. His message to them was: *Remember how great and how awesome our God is—even in the face of fear and criticism.*

He reminded them not to depend on their own strength but on God's power. They weren't doing this by their own power; they were doing it through God's power. *"Now to Him who is able..."* That's not talking about *your* power. It's not about *my* power, either. It's about *God's* power and *God's* strength.

Yes, I may need to stand up and fight—but He's going to fight with me. He's going to empower me. Why? Because I went to Him in prayer. Sometimes, I have to pivot. But I must remember how faithful He's been in the past—and trust that He'll be faithful in the future.

## Remember God's Track Record

Nehemiah reminded God's people, just as I'm reminding you:

- Remember the Red Sea, where God turned the sea into a highway.
- Remember the wilderness, where He fed His people daily.
- Remember the cloud by day and the fire by night that led them to the Promised Land.
- Remember the walls of Jericho—every time they made a turn, they had to *look back* at where God split the sea. And with every mocking voice from the walls, they could still say, *God, You did it then. You'll do it now.*
- Remember Gideon and his 300 men.
- Remember David—a teenager overlooked by his father. But full of faith, filled with the Holy Ghost, and willing to pick up five smooth stones. He said, *Today, giant, I'm going to kill you.*

Step out in faith and *remember* who your God is.

> When our enemies heard that we were aware of their
> plot and that God had frustrated it, we all
> returned to the wall, each to our own work.

> — Nehemiah 4:15

## Don't Forget to Remember

When they remembered God's faithfulness, they began to praise Him—and as they praised Him, God showed up. Don't forget to *remember*:

- Who you were before Christ.
- What it felt like to be hopeless, lost, bitter, and angry.
- What was it like before God gave you vision and purpose.
- What was it like before you became part of a family of faith.

We've traveled and seen incredible things. However, something happened in Honesdale, Pennsylvania. Something took place in this community of faith. Some of my preacher friends still ask, "What are you doing out there?" I respond, "Following God."

Some have even said, "We'd love for you to take over our ministry—we believe you could carry it further than we can. We want you to pick it up where we've left off." I'm honored by that. But my response is always the same: "Right now, God has me in Honesdale. If He says go, we'll go. But at this moment, He says stay—so we're staying right here until He comes back or calls us home."

## Your Past Is Fuel for Your Future

Maybe you're not exactly where you want to be, but that's okay. Just remember—you're also not where you used to be. Every time the enemy throws opposition your way, look him in the face and say: "Oh yeah, Devil? That's where I was. But look where I am now, and just watch where I'm going."

## God Was There Then—He'll Be There Again

God has blessed us abundantly. Our business is blessed. Our family is blessed. Why? Because of our obedience.

I remember what God has done. How about you? Do you remember...

- How He brought you through the fire—and you weren't burned.
- When He told you, *Keep your mouth shut.* It wasn't easy, but you did. And God strengthened relationships that were *meant* to stay.
- Remember when He removed people from your life who were a hindrance.

A prophet in my life once told me, "You don't need to explain anything to me. God already spoke. This is a season of exposure. Stay faithful. God will clear the path." And He did. If you're willing to stand firm and keep remembering what God has done, He'll bring you through your fire, too.

## Faith for Tomorrow

My past fuels my confidence. I know in whom I have believed, and I am fully persuaded He will do exactly what He said. As Billy Graham used to say: "I don't know what the future holds, but I know who holds the future. And because He lives, I can face tomorrow."

# Chapter Fifteen

## Building Something Lasting

"In all that has happened to us, you have remained righteous; you have acted faithfully, while we acted wickedly. Our kings, our leaders, our priests and our ancestors did not follow your law; they did not pay attention to your commands or the statutes you warned them to keep. Even while they were in their kingdom, enjoying your great goodness to them in the spacious and fertile land you gave them, they did not serve you or turn from their evil ways.

"But see, we are slaves today, slaves in the land you gave our ancestors so they could eat its fruit and the other good things it produces. Because of our sins, its abundant harvest goes to the kings you have placed over us. They rule over our bodies and our cattle as they please. We are in great distress.

"In view of all this, we are making a binding agree-

ment, putting it in writing, and our leaders, our
Levites and our priests are affixing their seals
to it."

— Nehemiah 9:33-38

## A Long-Term Vision for Generational Impact

When God gives you a vision, He provides a plan. When we collaborate, even when facing opposition, we can create something enduring—for Him. What is a church? It's something we build to last for generations. It's meant to continue reaching people, generation after generation. Witnessing the Lord's generational blessing is powerful—that's the heart of the matter. It's about building a church for everyone, at every stage of life. I believe God has a purpose and a plan for every season of life for those who remain willing and open to Him.

Anyone can start something. But enduring through tough times and not giving up when things get hard sets people apart. When your marriage, family, or health—whatever it is—faces difficulties, can you stand firm?

It's easy to receive, but can you give? Celebrating is enjoyable, but can you also make sacrifices? Are you built to last? These are crucial questions.

Our church is located in Wayne County, Pennsylvania, and one of the things I love about the people here is that they are built to last. I love this area—Honesdale has been wonderful. Before we arrived, people warned me, "Oh, they've chewed up men of God and spit them out." In response, I said, "We're the Thrive Tribe. We're ready to build and stay for the long haul." Why? Because we have the hope of glory living inside us.

We're not called to a short-term vision; He has given us a long-term one. Christmas Eve 2024 marked four years since our first service. In 2020, the building was a mess. We did everything we could to prepare. We had a vision in our hearts, and we pressed in through prayer. "God, give us a plan. Show us how." It was uncomfortable for a while, and even painful at times. But we believed He was calling us to step out in faith.

God's vision isn't only for our generation—it's also for future generations. He's the God of Abraham, Isaac, and Jacob. He's the God of every generation.

At a recent service, I noticed that our Thrive Kids filled the first three rows. We're creating a church for everyone. It's incredible what God is doing in Thrive Youth right now.

For the past two years, we have hosted a local kids' Christmas concert in our building. The school told me, "Pastor, you have the nicest venue in the area." Four years prior, the same building was to be demolished. But God does great things through people who catch His vision and work willingly in collaboration.

## Breaking the Short-Term Mindset

We need to shift our mindset from living for the temporary to focusing our hearts on the eternal. This isn't just about buildings or Sundays; it's about building God's Kingdom. We're not just building for today—we're building for future generations.

Nehemiah sacrificed so that others could benefit. Similarly, we give sacrificially—through tithes, offerings, and hard work—so that others can benefit now and in future generations.

When studying Nehemiah, we ultimately see Jesus. Two thousand years ago, Jesus made the ultimate sacrifice so we could reap its benefits. Today, we are the beneficiaries of His obedience.

# Chapter Sixteen

## Concern Creates a Vision—Not What Is, But What Can Be

### A Frustration That Sparked a Calling

A God-given vision often emerges from frustration with the status quo, sparking passion for what could be.

When we first saw the property where our church is now located, I felt frustrated. Having been born and raised in the Assemblies of God denomination, I knew that the building used to be an Assemblies of God church. Every time I drove by, my frustration grew. Do you know why? The building had been badly neglected and did not reflect the glory of an amazing God.

A few years ago, the presbyter from the Assemblies of God paid a visit. For some reason, he wanted my opinion—I probably wasn't the best person to ask. He asked, "How do you think we're doing?" By "we," he meant the Assemblies of God regarding their mission in the local area.

I was eager to share, "Well, brother, I'm glad you asked. I'll be honest with you. Something has been frustrating me for a while. I believe God is El Shaddai—He is the God of More Than Enough. He is Jehovah-Jireh—My God who will supply every one of our needs. God is exactly who He says He is, and I've seen Him prove it time and time again. However, I see a problem in our area. It appears to me that God is homeless in Honesdale. To me, that rundown building is embarrassing; I think we can do better than that."

He looked at me and said, "Really? Wouldn't it be amazing if God did something with *you* in that place?"

## The Birth of a Vision

I kept riding past the rundown building with a tree growing from it. Each time, I felt the Holy Spirit come over me. I talked about it with my dad and another friend. They both said, "You've got to take this on." But I had strong and clear objections: "That is not what I want to do. I'm enjoying a great life—we're traveling, preaching in different places, having fun. I don't want to be in Honesdale."

However, sometimes, when something frustrates you, it's actually God trying to birth something within you—not for what is, but for what it could become. Maybe that irritation is the very thing God has called you to make a difference in.

## Nehemiah's Example: A Heart for People

Nehemiah wasn't weeping over broken walls; he was weeping over broken people.

When we unite behind a vision, like building in Honesdale, we're not giving just because of a need for bricks and sticks. We give because we care about what God cares about—people who are far from Him.

# Chapter Seventeen

## From Concern to Clarity

### Prayer Brings a Plan

Nehemiah's concern sparks a vision, leading him to clarity. For four months, Nehemiah dedicates himself to prayer. When we go into our prayer closet with a concern, God provides clarity—He will give us a plan.

Many times, when God gives you a vision, it doesn't require immediate action, but it almost always calls for immediate patience. Sometimes, the hardest part is waiting for His direction. How's it going to happen, Lord? When will it happen? God, we're in the eleventh hour here. If You want to show up now, that would be okay.

We must learn that waiting is working. When we wait on God, He will always fulfill His promises.

> I was young and now I am old,
>   yet I have never seen the righteous forsaken
>   or their children begging bread.

They are always generous and lend freely;
   their children will be a blessing.

— Psalm 37:25-26

Nehemiah emerges from his prayer closet with clarity and a plan. When you leave your prayer closet, you should have a clear understanding of your plan.

I meet people all the time who say, *Someday, I'm going to have money.* Wonderful. That's a great vision. But what's your plan? How about getting a job? Start somewhere.

*Someday I'm going to retire a millionaire.* That's a great goal! But what's your plan to get there? What are you investing in today? What are you saving today? How are you sowing today?

*Someday, I'll own a business.* Wonderful. What's your plan to get there?

*I have a vision to be physically fit.* That's great too. But unless you get up off the sofa, brother, those stretchy pants will keep stretching in the wrong direction.

You need a plan. It might sound too simple, but it's true: a vision without a plan is only a fantasy.

## Vision That Impacts Generations

Everything I do with my business is for my kids. However, people don't always understand that.

Somebody recently told me, "I don't understand why you started the trash hauling business."

My answer was simple: "If the Lord should tarry, it's going to bless my children. That's why."

When you get a vision for your children—and what their future might be like—you put a plan into motion. You start saving for retirement. You begin investing for your future. You start sowing into the Kingdom of God because you realize it will have an impact for generations to come.

Nehemiah's concern gives him a vision. Through prayer, he gains clarity. But once he arrives in Jerusalem, he realizes the immensity of the task. He starts asking questions like: God, how am I going to rebuild these walls alone? How am I going to restore these burned-down gates by myself? He sees the people living amid the rubble. They walk over the flattened walls every day on their way to work, school, and everywhere else. They've learned to live with the debris. *God, how am I going to convince these people to help me?* he asked. But now, standing there in Jerusalem, Nehemiah realizes something powerful: He will need a whole community because this God-given vision is just too big for one man.

# Chapter Eighteen

## Every God-Given Vision Requires More Than Just You

### Vision Requires Community

When I started working on the church building rehab project, my good friend was there to help me right from the very beginning. He's talented, hardworking, and always ready to step in wherever he's needed. When we began the rehab project, God gave me the vision. I had the plan. But I needed others to collaborate with me to bring it to life.

We worked tirelessly through many nights. We did whatever it took because we had a vision in our hearts, a plan in our hands, and a willingness to work together. And we're just getting started.

Community is vital because every God-given vision needs more than one person; it always requires others. When Nehemiah returned to Jerusalem, he needed more than just the king's favor. While that was helpful, it wasn't enough. He had to cast a vision to a crowd of people living in ruins. He needed to delegate responsibilities, recruit a team, and empower the people to do the work.

That was the only way the wall would be rebuilt—everyone had to play their part.

We see community reflected in our own church. Thrive Church isn't great because of the building. It's not the lights or the sound system. It's the people—those willing to do their part. We have a healthy church; however, without the people, it would just be a lifeless building.

From the moment you pull onto our church property, faithful people are serving:

- People direct traffic and help you cross the street safely.
- People slow down drivers with lights on their cars.
- People arrive early to turn on the lights and air conditioning.
- People practice the drums during the week, sing, and prepare to lead us in worship.
- People greet you with a handshake and a smile, making you feel welcome in God's house.

These things are essential. It's how a community unites to achieve a shared vision.

I thank God for our ushers and the security team that keep everyone safe. I also thank God for the media team, the worship team, and the prayer team—people who know how to reach Heaven with their prayers.

I thank God for the people who have given in the past, continue to give now, and will give in the future. We wouldn't be here without them. Those first couple of years were difficult. Many times, Carolyn and I gave everything we had just to keep things going. Most people have no idea what we endured—or the sacrifices we made to push forward. But it was worth it every step of the way.

I'm grateful for the faithful people at the café, those who help with Communion Sundays, and those who took the lead in launching the Nicholson location. I also appreciate Thrive Kids and everyone with a heart to serve them. Thank God for Thrive Youth and the enthusiasm they bring. Thank God for those who recognize needs and step forward to meet them.

I'm grateful for the people who design merch because, honestly, I don't have a creative bone in my body when it comes to that. Thank God for everyone willing to do their part.

## Staying Rooted: Collaboration Creates Multiplication

Most people don't realize what's happening in Honesdale—the place where they said it couldn't be done.

*There's no money over there.* God's got all the money in the world. I'm not worried about that.

*They'll chew you up and spit you out.* I've got the Thrive Tribe standing with me.

*How are you going to do that?* Don't worry about it—I've got friends in high places. Garth Brooks might've had them in low places, but I've got mine in heavenly ones.

When we all collaborate, that's how the vision grows. We'll keep expanding until God reveals the next step to us. And when He does, we'll willingly advance even more. Until then, we'll keep moving forward.

# Chapter Nineteen

## The Bigger the Vision, The Bigger the Opposition

### Thriving Through Unity

Nehemiah's community began to build. However, when you start building, you often face opposition; the bigger the vision, the greater the opposition. Nehemiah teaches us how to handle criticism and opposition:

- First, go to God in prayer.
- Second, pivot. A pivot is a change of strategy, not a change of vision.
- Third, remember God's past faithfulness as fuel for your future.

When God gives you a vision and you start developing a plan, even gathering people, what most often thwarts the work of God's vision? Opposition, including disagreements over strategy, execution, and petty jealousy and backbiting.

I told my dad one day, "You know what, Dad? Pastoring in Honesdale has changed me in so many ways. Whatever hardships we've gone through, this has been the crown jewel in our lives." I truly meant it.

I love ministering at Thrive Church more than anything else. I'm probably Thrive's biggest cheerleader. This vision, this plan, and this collaboration—even the opposition—have brought me great joy. It feels like a fresh wind. I've been on big platforms. I've preached all over. I'm thankful for those experiences—but this vision, this place, and these people—they've touched me in a much deeper way.

## Focus on What Unites Us

*"People don't work together over there,"* the naysayers said. Well, they sure do here.

Before we started Thrive, I hardly knew some of the people who joined us. However, I shared the vision with them, and they believed in it by faith. It's incredible what God can accomplish when people work together. If we've achieved this much in just four years, what could we accomplish in the next four? Or in the next forty if the Lord tarries? I'm all in.

Many churches fall apart because they focus on differences. But here, we focus on what we agree on. We focus on collaboration over opposition. This church is diverse—and I love it. Heaven is going to be a diverse place, you know. I'm not chasing after a denomination. I just want to be part of God's kingdom.

There will never be a perfect church. But we do serve a perfect God—a God who sent His perfect Son to die for us. A God with a vision to redeem us. A God who didn't just have a vision but also a plan—named Jesus. A God willing to collaborate with humanity, even when opposition stood in the way. God sent His Son to build something that will last forever—and we are privileged to be part of it.

# Chapter Twenty

## Once Conflict Is Handled, The Vision Can Move Forward

### The Body of Christ at Work

If you learn to push past conflict, you can build something powerful for God. But too often, conflict steps in. Conflict creeps into marriages. Instead of strengthening strong relationships, it pushes people apart. You're trying to build a great family and leave a legacy for God, but conflict undermines your vision. Maybe you're working to build a business— we've built a couple of them, by God's grace—but conflict always steps in.

But here's the key: if you push through the conflict, you can stay focused on the vision and create something that lasts.

This principle not only speaks to the heart of every church, but it also applies to individuals. It relates to marriages, families, raising children, growing a business, managing households, excelling at work, and engaging within a church—for the glory of God.

It's remarkable that once construction started in Nehemiah's time, the wall was finished in only fifty-two days. Why? Because everyone worked together. Collaboration speeds up the vision.

When we work together, we can accomplish remarkable things for God. I believe God wants to operate within your family. How will this happen? By everyone doing their part—together.

I love seeing people in our church praying for our kids. We have grandparents praying for Thrive Youth—even if they don't have a teenager in the program. I told one of them recently, "Keep praying. You're making a difference."

Some people serving in Thrive Littles or Thrive Kids don't even have children of their own; some were never able to have kids. Through this community of faith, they have found a way to invest in the spiritual formation of a new generation. That's the body of Christ, and that's what church should look like.

People use their gifts, talents, and abilities to worship and serve collectively. Together, we build a church, start businesses, strengthen marriages, and raise godly families. Together, we make a difference in this community.

## A Legacy That Builds Others

Not long ago, I visited my friend Dwayne for the last time. He was one of the strongest men I've ever known—a real man's man. He taught me everything from digging a hole with a shovel to operating heavy equipment.

Dwayne was saved in 1995 at the old Peckville Assemblies of God church and had an incredible testimony—multiple marriages, a hard life—but was gloriously redeemed.

He donated trucks, equipment, time, and energy to help build God's kingdom. Dwayne used to tell me, "Tyler, everything in life is work—except when I'm on God's property. That's when peace comes over me."

He helped shape the man I am today. He taught me about trucks, machines, and sometimes about making a mess—but also about how to rebuild. Those skills allowed me to build God's house. Thank God for people like Dwayne, who were willing to pass down something to the next generation.

As iron sharpens iron, so one man sharpens another. Dwayne's gift wasn't preaching, but he passed along what he had. May we be people who do the same: pass along our faith, wisdom, and gifts to build something that lasts.

## Relationships Are the Framework for Building

I thank God for the board members of our church. There's no bickering, no fighting, and no drama. They're not just "yes men"— they're men of wisdom and integrity. They've managed our finances well, not because they're showy, but because they know how to steward what's been entrusted to them. And if a man can manage his own house well, he'll help manage God's house effectively. They love their wives and the Lord. I'm surrounded by great men—men who sometimes want to wrestle me down.

Some of these men wouldn't be here if we hadn't started Thrive Church. Two men were introduced to me during a message I gave on vision several years ago. I told everyone before me, "God has given me a vision to plant a church in Honesdale. I don't have a team. It's just Carolyn and me. But I believe God birthed this, and if anyone here is willing to help…"

What I didn't realize was that, at the same time, they were praying for God to intervene in that very area. They weren't even supposed to be at that service, and I wasn't supposed to be preaching. But they showed up, and so did I. Only God's hand could have orchestrated that. Now, they serve faithfully at our church. God knows exactly what He is doing.

## Relationships Start with Obedience

We have a talented and gifted person managing our sound and media—he does an excellent job. He's an introvert, which makes this story even more powerful.

A few years ago, his family went to California, and he showed up alone to church—which introverts usually don't do. After the service, he came over and said, "I really enjoyed the message." I responded, "Thank you. I'm Tyler."

Then he asked, "Would you have time to grab coffee this week?" It was a big step of faith for him, since he had never met me.

We met for coffee, and since then, he's been with me almost every Sunday. We've vacationed together, boated together, grilled steaks, and had three-hour conversations about leadership, Thrive's future, and our growth plans for the coming years. All of this started because one man took a step of faith.

## Community Grows When People Invest

I don't make these people show up. I don't pay them to be here. God has placed a vision in their hearts, and now, they're serving, giving, and encouraging—cheering me on from the front row. We're doing life together—sharing meals and hanging out at each other's houses.

It's more than a church; it's a family of faith. As we grow bigger, we will also become closer. No one is left behind. No one is missing. No one is broken.

When people work together, the vision accelerates. What God begins, He directs. God brings the right people at exactly the right moment. That's the beauty of a spiritual family; it endures longer than anything else.

## The Power of Sacrifice and the Promise of Completion

Each year, our church receives a special Vision offering—it's not what is required of us; it's what is over and above.

Why? Because I want to see this movement accelerate. There's always work to do. We need to train leaders. We must develop, grow, and expand. Why? Because we have to reach more people. We're never finished—we're always just getting started.

How will these goals be achieved? By everyone doing their part. And I believe—if God started it, God will finish it.

> He who began a good work in you will be faithful to
> bring it to completion in Christ Jesus our Lord.
>
> — Philippians 1:6

He is the Author, Perfecter, and Finisher of our faith. He is the Author and Perfecter of Thrive Church. Even in seasons of uncertainty, He remains the Finisher of Thrive Church.

He authored the marriage you're holding onto, and He will perfect it. Even when it looks like it's falling apart, He is the one who will finish it.

The family you're building—God is the one who gave you the vision. He perfects it through your prayers and sacrifices. He will see it through to the end.

The business that lives as a dream in your heart? He is the Author, Perfecter, and Finisher of your business. With God, all things are possible. What He started, He will finish. He will equip us every step of the way, just as He has in the past.

But I'm not only looking back—I'm also looking forward. I feel excited in my spirit for what's coming next.

We're going to achieve something great—and we're going to do it together. It's not about equal amounts; it's about equal sacrifice. It's about God speaking to each of us and our obedience to Him.

# Chapter Twenty-One

## People Must Assume Responsibility

### From Rebuilding Walls to Restoring Hearts

After Nehemiah 9, the walls are finished—but the next four chapters show what life is like after the building work stops. Nehemiah knew something important: you can rebuild the outside, but if you ignore the inside, it's only a matter of time before everything collapses.

It's like putting lipstick on a pig—it might look dressed up, but at the end of the day, it's still a pig. You can polish the outside and make it seem impressive, but if you don't tackle the root issue—if you don't address what's really going on inside—it won't last. We serve a God who changes us from the inside out. He works in our hearts, and He works in our lives.

We live in an era that celebrates the fake. What you see on social media isn't real life. Some people you meet in person are unrecognizable compared to their online image. They've created so much AI—edited photos, fake environments, and artificial versions of themselves. We're obsessed with appearance. But Scripture reminds us: "Man looks at the outward appearance, but God looks at the heart" (1 Samuel 16:7). If you don't deal with what's happening inside—in your marriage, your family, and your business—it's only a matter of time before the cracks appear. No matter how polished it looks on the outside, it will eventually fall apart.

## Responsibility Is the Foundation

If you want to build something that lasts, you have to take responsibility. That's not a popular idea today, but it comes directly from the Word of God. God expects us to be responsible—for our actions, our calling, and sometimes, even for burdens that weren't originally ours. God has given us a burden for Honesdale.

In Nehemiah 9, the people not only confessed their sin but also took ownership of the mess they had inherited. They didn't just blame their ancestors or their circumstances. They declared, "We'll take it from here. We'll own it and make it right."

Here's the truth: responsibility finds a way; irresponsibility finds an excuse. You've heard the saying, "Everything rises and falls on leadership." That means both the credit and the complaints land there. Whether they caused the problem or not, a responsible person says, "I'll step in. I'll help rebuild and restore."

I don't want to live with a mindset that says, *Well, I'm okay. My family's okay. I'm blessed. Jesus checked in with me on Sunday, and I'm on my way to Heaven.* I want more. I want to carry a burden for people who are far from God. I want to take responsibility for the broken, the lost, and those who need Jesus. Because if we don't—who will?

## Excuses or Responsibility?

Our church building sat unused for years—three dilapidated structures wasting away. Now, we have two beautiful buildings raised up to the glory of God. Why? Because we didn't just receive a vision—we embraced the responsibility to live for something greater than ourselves.

If you're irresponsible, you'll always find an excuse. That's what politicians do—blame the last person, blame the next, and blame anyone but themselves. However, biblical responsibility works differently. God calls us not only to take responsibility for our mistakes but also to accept responsibility for the outcomes we desire.

Take, for example, the topic of physical fitness. I dislike going to Planet Fitness every January. That's when everyone suddenly decides, "This is my year." Some stick with it longer than others, but eventually, the crowd disappears. Why does this happen every year in January? Because people make resolutions but never follow through.

You can talk about getting in shape, but unless you take responsibility, nothing will change. Vision without responsibility remains just a fantasy.

The same goes for marriage. You might say you want a good marriage, but you must take responsibility for working on it. You could say you want to be part of a life-giving church or see revival in your city, but are you doing your part to help make it happen?

## Giving That Reflects Responsibility

In Nehemiah 10, the people not only confess their sins but also take responsibility.

"We assume the responsibility for carrying out the
commands to give a third of a shekel each year for
the service of the house of our God."

— Nehemiah 10:32

They're not just talking about it—they're funding it. They're putting their resources into supporting God's work, going beyond the tithe to make sure God's house has what it needs.

"We also assume responsibility for bringing to the
house of the Lord each year the firstfruits of our
crops and of every fruit tree."

— Nehemiah 10:35

That's the heart I pray to have: God, make me a pillar of generosity in Your kingdom. I'm not trying to be a celebrity preacher or the next Billy Graham. I want to be faithful. I want to go where others won't, do what others won't do, and give what others won't give. I want to take responsibility where others have walked away.

## Stop Waiting—Start Acting

Nehemiah didn't just wait for a miracle. He prayed to God and then took action to become the miracle himself. That's a key difference. Some Christians are simply lazy and blame their problems on God.

*I'm just waiting on a miracle.* That's an excuse. Stop blaming God while you sit on your hands. Work as if it depends on you, while you pray as if it depends on Him. Meet Him in the middle and see what He'll do.

It's not our job to figure everything out. It's our job to start working. Say, "God, I'm going to make a difference. I'm going to be faithful with what I have—my time, my talent, and my treasure—and I trust You will take care of the rest." Be the miracle someone is praying for. Show up even when you don't feel like it. Give even when it hurts. Why? Because we're called to be faithful.

## Revival Starts with Responsibility

Our church is a miracle. If you'd seen where we started, you'd say, "Amen." Nothing looked like it does now. Drug addicts lived on the third floor, sleeping on haystacks and surrounded by needles. Now, three neglected buildings are beautiful and functional—thanks to people taking responsibility.

Remember the story of the Good Samaritan? Many people walked past. My prayer is, "If I see a problem, make me the solution. If I'm not the solution, show me who is." I don't just want to pray for a miracle—I want to be one.

It's important to pray for revival—and we should. But at some point, you need to take action to ignite the revival. Too many people just sit back, pray, and never do anything.

Souls won't be saved unless someone goes (Romans 10). We could have easily passed on starting our church. In 2020, life was good—traveling, preaching, and raising a baby. But God stirred our hearts.

I knew it would cost us—time, money, and nearly everything we had. But God asked, "Will you assume the responsibility?" And we did.

## The Weight and Reward of Responsibility

If you want a great church, a great marriage, a strong family, lasting friendships, or a successful business, you must take responsibility. Everyone wants to be the boss—until challenges arise. Easy days of smooth sailing are common. But when things fall apart, money gets tight, or things aren't going well, that's when real leadership appears. That's when those willing to bear the burden stand out.

When God established our church in Honesdale, He didn't just give us a building; He entrusted us with a responsibility. I refuse to pass that responsibility to anyone else. Maybe it's how I'm wired. I want to carry what God asked me to carry.

The truth is, when God gives someone an assignment, He often gives it to several people. But not everyone says yes. I believe God called others to come here and do this, but they didn't respond. I've told God, "Send somebody else." And He replied, "I've tried." So we stepped in. We said yes. We assumed the responsibility.

## A Vision Worth the Weight

We didn't add a second service solely because I needed something else to do. By the end of a Sunday, I'm worn out. But I took on the responsibility. We're going to reach people far from God—even if it means preaching twice, five times, or ten times. It's not about comfort; it's about creating something that lasts.

Every empty seat represents an opportunity—an invitation—to take responsibility for another soul. This is our church. This is God's house. We all have a part to play. Be the person who stands up and says, "I'll carry the weight. I'll answer the call. I'll do my part." Imagine what God will do with that—a person willing to take responsibility and build something that will stand the test of time.

# Chapter Twenty-Two

## Create Accountability

### Accountability Binds Us Together

When I talk about accountability, I'm referring to helping and equipping one another as a church community to live out our shared values. Accountability is the bond that connects commitment to results. Yes, it can reveal problems—but it also encourages growth. Accountability isn't only about "making sure you're not slipping and dipping into sin." I understand that view, but there's also a growth-oriented kind of accountability.

Most people won't go to the gym on their own initiative. Maybe you will, but most people perform better with accountability. That's one reason I love the Bible reading plan we do as a church. We read through the Bible each year, and it provides a healthy form of accountability. We value the Word of God—His highest authority on Earth. When we read together, it's not about pointing out, *Hey, you didn't read today.* It's the opposite. It's about encouragement. It fosters healthy, spiritual accountability—and that's powerful.

A woman from our church reached out to me and said, "Pastor, I can't tell you how grateful I am that we read the Bible together each year. I was born and raised in church and was even married to a pastor, but I never read the entire Bible in a year. Now, I've done it three years in a row. I'm even ahead of schedule." Why? Because we built accountability around something we value.

## What Accountability Is—and What It Isn't

Healthy accountability helps us grow stronger. But it's not about calling someone at midnight to confess your sins of the day. That's not helpful accountability—that's disruptive. I'm not a Catholic priest, nor am I Jesus. Call on Him at midnight if you need to. There's a time and place for serious conversations during struggles. True accountability means, *Here are the gaps in my life. Can you walk with me as I grow?* It's life-giving, honest, and mutual.

Nehemiah modeled real accountability.

> "In view of all this, we are making a binding agreement, putting it in writing, and our leaders, our Levites and our priests are affixing their seals to it."
>
> — Nehemiah 9:38

He clarified their beliefs and values. He established accountability. Later, in Nehemiah 10:39, he emphasizes it: "We will not neglect the house of our God." Because the last time they neglected the house of God—when people didn't tithe, didn't give, and didn't live out their values—the entire city was overtaken.

Let me ask you—who comes first? Is it you or God? Is it your house or His house? Is it your dream or His dream? I don't want my dreams to come true. I want God's dreams for my life. I don't want my desires; I want His desires. If you aim to walk in these things, you must build accountability.

## Don't Follow Your Heart—Follow God's

We live in a generation that says, "Just follow your heart." No, don't follow your heart. Jeremiah said, *"The heart is deceitful above all things and beyond cure. Who can understand it?"* (Jeremiah 17:9).

*Just follow your heart.* Look where that's gotten us. It's not about following your heart—it's about following God's heart. It's about asking, "God, where are You leading me? How are You guiding me? What are Your values?" This is how we build a community of responsibility. As a community of believers within a church, we can say, "These are our values as a church, this is what we believe, and this is what we hold ourselves accountable to."

Nehemiah essentially says, *Let's not neglect the house of God, because the world around us depends on it.*

## Building amid Resistance

The year 2020 was a wild ride for us—and it had nothing to do with COVID-19. We started with a plan and faced plenty of opposition. Still, we kept moving forward, working together, and trusting in God. Honestly, it was a big challenge to get Thrive Church off the ground.

Some people believe, *if God is with you, there won't be any challenges.* Really? Show me that in Scripture. *If it's hard, it must not be God.* Wrong again. It is very biblical to face challenges; what is unscriptural is to live defeated.

The greater the attack and the greater the opposition, the greater the blessing. I feel this with every fiber of my being.

To start Thrive Church, Carolyn and I made significant sacrifices. Why? Because people matter. The world around us depends on this work.

People sometimes look at our lives and say, "Must be nice." But they don't understand the price we've paid or the effort we've invested. I challenge you—work as I have, sacrifice as we have, and you'll see what God can do in your life as well.

Everyone notices the harvest, but no one sees the seeds that were sown. What remains is jealousy, along with a lack of understanding and appreciation for the process behind the harvest.

## One Life Worth the Cost

We held our very first service on December 24, 2020. It was meant to be a simple event in a building we rented just for that day—a Christmas gathering to let the community know, "Hey, we're here. Jesus is here. We're starting a church."

The following weekend, I was away with my family. During some free time, I was scrolling through my phone when I came across a testimony that stopped me in my tracks. I don't get choked up often, but that day, I did.

A woman shared, "Four years ago today, they were planning my funeral. I had checked myself into rehab one last time, completely bound by addiction. I had five kids. I was young, broken, and barely surviving."

Her sister told her, "There's a new church in town. You need a fresh start. Please come with me." She hesitated. "I can't go," she said. "I'm withdrawing. I'm a wreck." But her sister kept at her, and finally, she agreed.

She recalled, "Every word preached that night hit me like a sledge-hammer. It felt like God was speaking directly to me." That night—December 24, 2020 —became her turning point. She continued, "That was the night God found me. My kids got their mom back. My husband got his wife back. My father got his daughter back."

She explained that she'd already lost her mother to addiction, and other family members had gone through the same loss. But that night, her story had taken a new turn.

As we drove home, I called my dad and said, "Call the owner. Tell him I need that building every Sunday from now on. Whatever it takes—make it happen."

Why? Because of just one person—one life changed. That's all I could think about. Just that one life—and how God had used us to reach her.

## Values That Drive the Mission

Thrive Church is a place where everyone is always welcomed. Even if you're distant from God, you're still welcomed here. I believe God can transform anyone—any hurt, any habit, and any hang-up.

I don't care what it costs me. I'm all in. God's been good to us. What I want more than anything is to reach people far from God.

We truly stand by our values:

- Jesus is our message.
- People are our heart.
- Generosity is our privilege.

- Honor is our calling.
- Excellence is our spirit.
- Servant leadership is our identity.
- Passion is our pursuit.

I was reflecting on that woman's testimony the other day, and it stirred something deep inside me. Do you know why? Because sometimes, you need to look back on God's faithfulness to find new strength for your faith moving forward.

Our church was never built by just one person; it was built by many who chose to take responsibility.

## Generosity Is a Privilege, Not an Obligation

You don't have to give—you get to give. Obedience involves bringing the tithe, but generosity goes beyond that. It's not about what's required; it's about what God prompts you to do. I hope this book has inspired you to serve God and His church with your whole heart. That's why this isn't just a book about giving; it's a book about vision—because that's the core of who we are. *God, I want to serve You fully. And I want to serve Your Church.* We were saved to serve. I've already answered the call to salvation, but I've also responded to the second call: the call to serve.

## We're Saved to Serve

This church has a strong backbone. We say, "We're saved to serve." We're not afraid to stand up in the face of adversity and declare, "People are worth it."

So I'm all in—my time, my talent, and my treasure.

What about you? You need to take responsibility and establish accountability. Are you ready to pray, plan, and collaborate on the vision God has given you? Are you prepared to unite with others, take responsibility, and build something that will last? God is always speaking; it's up to us to listen and have the faith to move forward.

# Afterword

This book has been about vision, but you can't have a true vision for your life without a relationship with Jesus. Maybe you don't know my Jesus. Today can be your day!

Heaven and Hell are real. Which one is your destination? The only way to reach Heaven is through the shed blood of Jesus Christ. *"Jesus is the way, the truth, and the life. No one can come to the Father except through Him"* (John 14:6). The only path to Heaven is through Him. You must accept Him by faith. Just as Nehemiah prayed a prayer of repentance, you need to repent of your sins. I'm not talking about going to speak to a priest in the confessional; I mean going directly to God with your repentance. The Bible says in 1 John 1:9, *"If we confess our sins, he is faithful and just to forgive us and cleanse us from all unrighteousness."* Romans 10:9 states: *"If you believe in your heart and confess with your mouth, you will be saved."* As Billy Graham often quoted: *"For what would it profit a man to gain the whole world, but forfeit his own soul?"* What would it profit Thrive Church to gain the whole world, but lose souls? This is all about souls. This is all about reaching people far from God.

Someday, as you stand before God, he'll either say to you, "Well done, thou good and faithful servant," or "Depart from me, I never knew you."

You know what I want to be said about me when I stand before Him? I don't want Him to say, "Oh, you're a great preacher," or "Oh, you did a good business thing," or "You took great care of your kids, you are a great husband and great dad." That's all well and fine. I want to be all those things. But what I want to hear when I'm found and stand before Him is that I was faithful. I want Him to say, "Tyler, every opportunity I gave you, you were faithful."

A while back, I said, *God, I think I could do this here. Moving stuff around, trying to put a plan together.* I heard Him whisper in my spirit, *Faithful. Faithful.* I said, *Lord, that's all I want to be. I just want to be faithful. I want to be a faithful servant.*

If you're not right with Jesus, you can take care of that right now, right where you are. It's not a prayer that saves; it's faith in Christ alone that saves. You can express your faith in Jesus by praying a prayer like this:

> Dear Jesus, I admit I am a sinner and need a savior. Jesus, I ask You to forgive me for my sins. I repent, and I accept You as my Savior and Lord. Heaven is real, and I will be there someday because of what You did for me. Thank You; my name is now written in the Lamb's Book of Life. Forgive me, Father. Receive me, Lord. I ask You to fill me with the power of the Holy Spirit. In Jesus' mighty name, Amen.

*Afterword*

# About Tyler Drost

**Pastor Tyler Drost** is the founding pastor of Thrive Church in Honesdale, Pennsylvania. Raised in a pastoral family, Tyler felt called to ministry early in life. After graduating from Northpoint Bible College, he and his wife, Carolyn, served at Peckville Assembly of God under the leadership of his father, Pastor Terry Drost.

In 2020, driven by a passion to reach underserved communities, Tyler and Carolyn launched Thrive Church Honesdale. This was followed by the founding of Thrive Church Nicholson in 2024 and Thrive Church Southwest Florida in 2025. Their mission is to bring hope, healing, and the life-changing message of Jesus Christ to Honesdale, the surrounding region, and beyond.

Tyler's ministry centers on spiritual growth, community engagement, and living a vision-driven life. Through dynamic preaching and a heart for outreach, he inspires people to discover and pursue the unique vision God has for them.

He and Carolyn live in Northeast Pennsylvania with their two children, dedicating their lives to building the local church and cultivating a vibrant, faith-filled community.

www.thrivechurchhonesdale.com

*Scan or Touch for Apple Podcast*

instagram.com/thrivechurch_honesdale
facebook.com/thrivehonesdale
tiktok.com/@thrive_church
youtube.com/@thrivechurchhonesdale3248